Frances Tenenbaum, Series Editor

HOUGHTON MIFFLIN COMPANY
Boston • New York 1999

Topiaries
& Espaliers

Plus other designs for shaping plants

Linda Yang

Copyright © 1999 by Houghton Mifflin Company
Text copyright © 1999 by Linda Yang
Drawings copyright © 1999 by Steve Buchanan

Taylor's Guide and *Taylor's Weekend Gardening Guides* are registered trademarks of
Houghton Mifflin Company.

Library of Congress Cataloging-in-Publication Data

Yang, Linda.
      Topiaries & espaliers : plus other designs for shaping plants / Linda Yang.
         p. cm. — (Taylor's weekend gardening guides)
      Includes index.
      ISBN 0-395-87516-1
      1. Topiary work. 2. Espaliers. 3. Hedges. 4. Knot gardens.
      I. Title. II. Series.
   SB463.Y35 1999
   715'.1 — dc21   98-39971
                                                            CIP

Printed in the United States of America.

WCT 10 9 8 7 6 5 4 3 2 1

Book design by Deborah Fillion
Cover photograph © by Scott Phillips/Kitchen Garden

CONTENTS

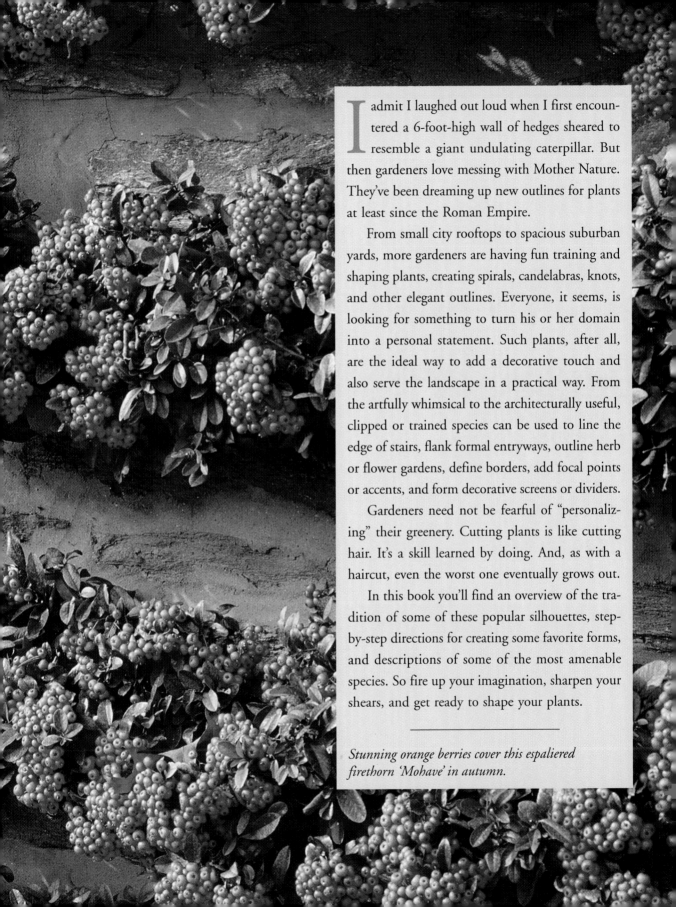

I admit I laughed out loud when I first encountered a 6-foot-high wall of hedges sheared to resemble a giant undulating caterpillar. But then gardeners love messing with Mother Nature. They've been dreaming up new outlines for plants at least since the Roman Empire.

From small city rooftops to spacious suburban yards, more gardeners are having fun training and shaping plants, creating spirals, candelabras, knots, and other elegant outlines. Everyone, it seems, is looking for something to turn his or her domain into a personal statement. Such plants, after all, are the ideal way to add a decorative touch and also serve the landscape in a practical way. From the artfully whimsical to the architecturally useful, clipped or trained species can be used to line the edge of stairs, flank formal entryways, outline herb or flower gardens, define borders, add focal points or accents, and form decorative screens or dividers.

Gardeners need not be fearful of "personalizing" their greenery. Cutting plants is like cutting hair. It's a skill learned by doing. And, as with a haircut, even the worst one eventually grows out.

In this book you'll find an overview of the tradition of some of these popular silhouettes, step-by-step directions for creating some favorite forms, and descriptions of some of the most amenable species. So fire up your imagination, sharpen your shears, and get ready to shape your plants.

Stunning orange berries cover this espaliered firethorn 'Mohave' in autumn.

CHAPTER 1
TIPTOP TOPIARY

For some folks, topiary and Disney are synonymous. I can't help chuckling at — but I also can't resist — those cute green mice, Mickey and Minnie, especially when they're topped with hats of blooming flowers. Topiary, the art of clipping and shaping plants to suit the whim of humans, has actually been around for many centuries, and it now includes quite an assortment of forms. Through the ages topiary has provided gardens — and gardeners — with a delightful range of live decorative sculpture.

Although the date of the first topiary is unknown, at least since ancient Rome gardeners have been beguiled by plants clipped and trained to "unnatural" forms. According to Pliny the Elder, the 1st-century Roman naturalist, it was not unusual for the *topiarius,* the gardener who trimmed the plants, to shear hedges into fanciful outlines. Pliny described entire green scenes depicting a hunt, a battle, and even a fleet of ships. The fall of Rome in the 5th century marked the demise of the grand villas along with their gardens, and as the Dark Ages descended, the decorative landscape disappeared.

It was not until the 12th or 13th centuries that the idea of clipping plants for beauty as well as utility reappeared. Cloistered monks used their monastery

*Regular clipping ensures that the
delightful features of a boxwood bear
are captivating and neat.*

courtyards for neat plantings of vegetables and herbs, and also trained and clipped fruiting trees. With the Renaissance and the rediscovery of the arts of classical Rome, elegance in the landscape returned. From Britain to Belgium, gardeners took to their shears, and green globes, spheres, urns, animals, and birds enhanced the outdoor scene once again.

TOPIARIES WITHOUT FRAMES

There are several ways of creating a topiary. One of the most popular is what I call the frameless method, as there's no "official" term for this style. This is a clipped plant that stands on its own feet (so to speak). While support might be required for the stem or trunk when the training begins or when the plant is very young, no other prop or frame is used for this sculptural form. The outline is strictly a result of the clipping artistry of the gardener.

A ROSEMARY LOLLIPOP

I have no scientific numbers to prove it, but I'd say that if there is a favorite shape for the frameless topiary, it's the playful, single-stemmed ball at the top of a stem popularly known as a lollipop (which is, after all, an apt description of its shape). Although I've outlined here the steps for making a lollipop topiary from a non-hardy plant like rosemary *(Rosmarinus officinalis),* you can also make it from hardy species (see Plants for Topiaries or Standards without Frames on page 12).

Step 1: Begin your lollipop rosemary by carefully looking over the nursery stock. Select a plant with a sturdy, reasonably straight stem. A distinctly upright stem or trunk is called a leader.

Step 2: Cut away all side leaves or branches (see figure A on page 5) along its lower stem, leaving only a single upright stem and several small side branches along the uppermost portion of the stem.

Step 3: Slide the plant from its nursery pail and plant it in an attractive container using any all-purpose potting soil. Choose a pot that's slightly larger than the one it was grown in and sturdy enough to support the plant without tipping.

Lollipop Topiary

A

B

C

D

E

The Standard

Don't be confused if you occasionally see what looks like a lollipop topiary referred to as a standard. The line between the two terms is certainly hazy, and more than one gardener insists they're the same. However, the word "standard" tends to be most popularly applied when flowering species, like geranium, fuchsia, or lantana, are trained to treelike forms. Such species are clipped loosely so that their heads are more moplike in appearance than ball-shaped. A too-tight clipping would remove their exquisite blooms.

The word standard is also used when nurserymen create a lollipop shape using a method known as grafting, instead of the training outlined on pages 5 and 6. In this case, a cascading or bushy species, such as a polyantha rose, is grafted (attached) to the top of the strong stem of a sturdy, upright species. This grafting method is used for various shrubs and trees including dogwoods, cherries, and crabapples as well as several kinds of evergreens.

'The Fairy' rose is renowned for its continual summer blooms. This topiary, with its informally clipped flowering head, is also known as a standard or tree rose.

Step 4: Once the plant is in place, firm the soil well and then insert close to the stem a slender but strong wood stake — a length of bamboo is ideal (see figure B on page 5). Cut it slightly shorter than the height you want your lollipop to reach. Using twist-ties or raffia, tie the stem securely to the stake, straightening it as you go.

Step 5: Allow this leader to grow and lengthen until the plant reaches several inches above the stake, or the height you desire. Then pinch or snip off the tip of the stems, leaving all the other top side shoots (see figure C). When these small stems have grown an inch or so, snip off their tips (see figure D). Soon thereafter, two small buds should appear. When each of these grows several sets of leaves, snip their tips (figure D on page 5). Continue to repeat this process until the lollipop head is a dense and well-developed ball (figure E on page 5).

A lollipop carved from a hardy yew is a year-round evergreen feature in this garden.

A poolside looks elegant with a three-tiered juniper poodle in a Greek urn.

A MYRTLE POODLE

Once you've mastered the rosemary lollipop with its single top ball, you can try a variation on the theme called the poodle. This is a lollipop with multiple balls, or tiers, along its stem. Most poodles have three, but you can try two, four, or any number that inspires you. You can again use a rosemary, or this time, try myrtle *(Myrtus communis)*.

Step 1: As with the rosemary lollipop, it's best to begin your myrtle poodle by looking over the nursery stock and choosing a plant with a sturdy, reasonably straight stem.

Step 2: Cut away all side leaves or branches along the stem except at the points where you want the tiers to form.

Step 3: Follow lollipop steps 3, 4, and 5 as noted earlier, snipping the tips of twigs around the tiers until these heads are dense and well developed (see figure D on page 5). Keep in mind that it's the repeated snipping of the growing tips that creates the glorious bushy shapes.

A YEW SPIRAL

I remember watching an expert nurseryman change a bushy yew shrub (and later, a fluffy rosemary) into a full-blown spiral in less than ten minutes. It was like watching a sheep-shearing contest — he was very fast and very secure in his every move. The rest of us, though, will move more slowly (and with a lot less confidence). However, it is no more difficult to create a spiral topiary than it is to create a lollipop or poodle. The final result simply looks more complex.

Step 1: As with the lollipop form, begin by selecting a Japanese yew *(Taxus cuspidata)* with a strong, straight stem. This time, however, choose a specimen that is also bushy and well branched along its entire height.

Step 2: Insert a stake into the soil close to the trunk and cut it at the height you want your finished plant to be. Secure the stem to the support in as straight a line as possible (see figure A on page 10).

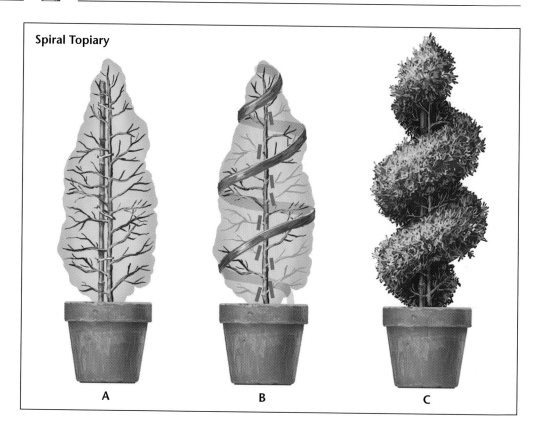

Spiral Topiary

A   B   C

Step 3: Now it's time to shear the spiral outline. Since your eye is unlikely to be as sure as that of that nurseryman I saw, you will need some help in clipping a neat line. The easiest guide for this silhouette is a long piece of cord or ribbon. Tack or tie it to the top of the stake and wind it down in a loose spiral around the plant, adjusting it so that the circular outline is even (see figure B above).

Step 4: Starting at the bottom of the plant and following the line of your guide, snip back to the trunk all the twigs that are beneath the cord. You will then have the spiral shape clearly defined. Once that's done, even out the remaining portions of twigs in between (see figure C above).

Step 5: As the plant continues to develop, secure the new stem or trunk to the stake and trim to maintain the shape. When the plant reaches the height you want, snip off the top of the leader.

A matched pair of spirals flank the end of a brick path.

A Yew Corkscrew

The corkscrew is a variation on the spiral. But in this case, the plant to select is one that's young enough to have a flexible stem.

Step 1: Plant your yew (either in the ground or a container) and then sink a sturdy stake into the soil next to it.

Step 2: Gently bend the stem and wind it around the stake. Secure the plant with ties or twist-ties so it remains in place.

Step 3: Snip or pinch off the tips of twigs and stems to create a neat outline. When the plant reaches the desired height, cut off the top of the vertical stem or leader.

Step 4: After some months (or years, depending on the rate of growth of your plant) your yew will mature sufficiently to develop a tough, self-supporting trunk and will hold the corkscrew shape itself. When that happens, slip out the stake and discard it.

Plants for Topiaries or Standards without Frames

Ilex crenata / **Japanese holly**
Sun or light shade
Zone 6
If you want that boxwood "look" but a truly hassle-free plant, choose from among the many little-leaved evergreen hollies. Although lacking the elegance and aroma of box, the small oval leaves of the Japanese holly *(I. crenata)* more than compensate by being exceedingly amenable to less than ideal conditions including heavy or dry soil and limited light. This plant and its many hybrids are also seemingly impervious to pests and disease. *I. glabra* 'Densa' is hardy to Zone 4.

*A carefully clipped boxwood basket appears
to be just another casual garden accessory,
belying its years of training and shaping.*

Asymmetrically clipped poodles with multiple tiers are symmetrically positioned in a small front garden.

Wire cables are used to position and train the limbs of a multistemmed poodle.

Laurus nobilis / Sweet bay
Sun or light shade
Zone 8
Having enjoyed my 2-foot-high houseplant, I was truly flabbergasted when I saw this native Mediterranean evergreen in its full glory as a 30-foot-tall lollipop. The laurel of ancient poets, its luxuriant oval dark green leaves are also a traditional ingredient in the classic bouquet garni of French cooking. The twigs are flexible when young but stiffen with age. Once established, this fragrant plant manages nicely with minimal water.

The bright spring growth of symmetrical plantings of Alberta spruce (Picea glauca) *enhance the elegance of the black painted lattice surrounding a terrace door.*

Myrtus communis / **Myrtle**
Sun or light shade
Zone 8
This shiny-leaved aromatic native of the Mediterranean tolerates both heat and drought. Its creamy white summer flowers are followed by blue-black autumn fruit. Although the species can grow 15 feet tall, diminutive cultivars with small leaves, like 'Microphylla', rarely exceed 2 feet. The variegated hybrids are less easily found but well worth a search.

A scented geranium is a fragrant multitiered topiary.

Pelargonium spp. / Geranium
Sun and light shade
Zone 10

The many members of this rather large South African genus, with their rangy habit and somewhat woody stems, are ideally suited for topiaries. Choices include the ordinary zonal geranium (of windowbox fame) and various ivy-leaved kinds (which resemble the English ivies). But my absolute favorites are the many dozens with deliciously scented and textured leaves. Fragrances include the aromas of nutmeg, cinnamon, apple, peppermint, lemon, and rose. Many bear clusters of small flowers in shades of pink, purple, and white.

Rhododendron spp. / Rhododendron and azaleas
Sun, part sun, and shade
Zones vary

The seemingly infinite members of the rhododendron genus — a group that includes the azaleas — offer an equally infinite number of leaf sizes and periods of bloom. Flower colors now vary beyond the previous limits of white to pink and purple, with yellows and golds available to brighten the scene. The little-leaved varieties are superb for topiary training. In most cases, moist, rich, acidic soil is preferred.

Which Plant Where — or Hardy Versus Tender

Gardeners have a special way of referring to plants that are considered amenable to cold weather conditions and to those that are not. Knowing which plants grow where can help you decide if the topiary or espalier of your dreams will survive a winter outside in your garden or is better planted in a container and brought indoors when it's cold.

Gardeners refer to plants as hardy if they tolerate extended periods of frost. A tough plant like Chinese juniper *(Juniperus chinensis)*, for example, has the relatively low Hardiness Zone number of 3 (see map on page 115). This means that a clipped or shaped Chinese juniper is likely to survive outdoors as far north as Zone 3 (or where winter days may dip to around -30 or -40°F).

Gardeners refer to plants as tender or nonhardy if they generally are *not* able to tolerate extended periods of frost. A plant like common myrtle *(Myrtus communis)*, for example, has the relatively high Hardiness Zone number of 8 to 9. This means that a clipped or shaped myrtle is likely to survive outdoors only to Zones 8 or 9 (or where winter days may dip to between +20 and +30°F.)

If your garden's climate is not reliably benign, it's prudent to grow nonhardy species in containers and keep them safely indoors through winter; if their roots are able to "survive," their foliage and stems may be so damaged that their decorative aspects are lost.

Since the plant possibilities for topiaries and espaliers are many and varied — and the amount of time, effort, and money invested can be considerable — I plant myself securely on the conservative side when choosing those to be kept outdoors all year.

A pink flowering azalea shaped to a two-tiered poodle adds color to a city scene.

Rosmarinus officinalis / Rosemary
Sun and light shade
Zone 8

Rosemary is for remembrance, or so the herbalists say. Remembrance, at least in the case of an indoor plant, means never forgetting to water. If you do, the leaves will drop and the plant will die. Fortunately, rosemaries are less fussy outdoors. A native of southern Europe, this aromatic gray-green plant has forms that are distinctly upright in their growing pattern, and other forms that are definitely recumbent. Variety names are often confused, so use your eye to select the plant whose shape fits your needs. When pruning, save your snippings for use in the kitchen. Rosemaries produce beautiful flowers, typically lavender and sometimes white. (But none has ever done so in my New York City garden or windowsill.)

A fanciful assortment of sheared outlines in contrasting green and gold foliage add color as well as architectural patterns to a formal walkway.

A spiral topiary is easily moved, thanks to its lightweight, faux ceramic container of fiberglass.

Neatly clipped lavender lollipops are formal anchors in a garden whose centerpiece is a mop-headed flowering tree.

ADDITIONAL PLANTS FOR TOPIARIES OR STANDARDS WITHOUT FRAMES

Zone 2   *Juniperus virginiana* / Eastern redcedar
Zone 5   *Cornus kousa* / Oriental dogwood
              Hibiscus syriacus / Rose of Sharon
              Lavandula angustifolia / Lavender
              Taxus cuspidata / Japanese yew
Zone 6   *Buxus microphylla* / Japanese boxwood
              B. sempervirens / English boxwood
Zone 7   *Camellia japonica* / Camellia
              Helicrysum angustifolium / Curry plant
Zone 8   *Abutilon hybridum* / Flowering maple or Chinese bellflower
              Aloysia triphylla / Lemon verbena
              Fuchsia spp. / Fuchsia
              Podocarpus macrophyllus / Yew pine
Zone 9   *Hibiscus rosa-sinensis* / Hibiscus or rose of China
Zone 10 *Coleus blumei* / Coleus
              Citrus spp./ Orange, lime, lemon
              Lantana camara / Lantana
              Nerium oleander / Oleander
Zones vary *Malus* spp. / Apple and crabapple
              Rosa spp. / Rose

TOPIARIES WITH FRAMES

In another major category of topiary, a frame or similar support is used. This category is best divided into two types, which I call the empty-frame method and the stuffed-frame method.

THE EMPTY-FRAME TOPIARY

In the empty-frame method, an artistically fashioned support gives shape to one or more plants. Plants with flexible limbs, such as rosemary, geranium, and trailing or vining species like ivy and jasmine, are planted at the base of the frame and then trained to grow up and around until the support is completely covered.

A simple design might be a flat outline traced to the shape of a heart or hoop, for example, or it could be a three-dimensional outline in the shape of a globe or a cone.

While the support may be a piece of flexible wood like bamboo or willow, a favorite of many topiary makers is wire because of its durability and many possibilities for creative work (see Getting Wired on page 33).

A TALL JASMINE CIRCLE

If the lollipop is the most popular frameless topiary form, then the tall circle (and its variations) is quite possibly the most popular topiary where an empty frame gives shape and support. Like the lollipop, the tall circle features a round form that sits a foot or more above the soil.

Step 1: Since the tall circle topiary starts with a frame, begin with a length of wire about 6 feet long. Bend the central portion of this wire into a circle measuring about a foot in diameter, with two long legs (see figure A on page 25). You can most easily achieve a perfect circular outline by using as a template an appropriately sized round pot or bowl.

TIPS FOR SUCCESS

PATIENCE IS A VIRTUE

You can't rush a topiary. Depending on the species, size of the plant you begin with, and type of topiary you are trying to create, it can take anywhere from six months to several years to develop the dense, well-formed, and bushy creation that will wow your friends. Be patient.

Step 2: Twist the legs around each other to create a straight and strong "stem." Assuming your topiary is planned for a container, make a sturdy support for the form by bending the two bottom pieces outward and around in opposite directions (see figure B on page 25).

Step 3: Prepare your container by placing a curved bit of crockery over the drainage hole at the bottom. Add a thin layer of all-purpose potting soil and set the frame in place. Holding it firmly, cover its base with enough soil to make it reasonably stable.

Step 4: Plant a bushy jasmine (*Jasminum officinale*) plant with its root ball as close to the center of the pot as possible. Continue adding soil to about a half-inch below the rim. Tamp firmly all around to stabilize both plant and frame.

Simple Empty Frame Topiaries

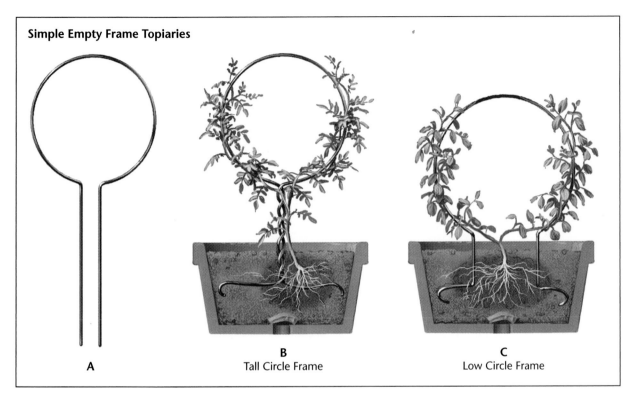

A

B
Tall Circle Frame

C
Low Circle Frame

Step 5: Get the plant stems going on their journey over the frame by securing them with twist-ties or raffia. Spread the strands as evenly as possible and remove oversized leaves or shoots.

Step 6: As the plant grows, tie the new shoots in place to cover the form. Clip wayward shoots regularly to keep the outline neat.

A LOW FUCHSIA HOOP

If the tall circle sits high above the soil, the low hoop appears to rise directly from the soil line.

Step 1: Begin with a length of wire about 5 feet in length. Bend the central portion of this wire into a circle measuring about $1\frac{1}{2}$ feet in diameter.

Step 2: Use the remaining lengths to form two short legs. Spread them apart, with the bottom pieces bent outward in opposite directions (see figure C on page 25).

Step 3: Prepare the container and plant a bushy fuchsia. Proceed as directed in steps 3, 4, and 5 on pages 24–25.

Once you've mastered the tall circle or the short hoop, you might enjoy trying your hand with some of the other charming and easily created framed variations, such as the heart or the fan.

A brilliant yellow-flowered florist's broom (Genista cariensis), *clipped as a mop-headed standard, nearly upstages a dark green English ivy trained on a circular wire frame.*

A prostrate rosemary, coaxed up and around a wire frame, is a distinctive living globe.

On this windowsill is a rhythmic array of rosemaries — rosemary circles and lollipops create an interesting display.

AN ENGLISH IVY SPIRAL

The spiral differs somewhat from the previous forms in that the frame has an added piece of support, a hollow length of bamboo stake.

Step 1: Begin by wedging a length of bamboo stake, about 1½ feet tall, into the drainage hole of the pot, placing it in as upright a position as possible. To keep it securely anchored, surround it with stones or coarse gravel (see figure A below).

Step 2: Gently pull a 7- or 8-foot coil of wire outward into a corkscrew or spire shape that's broader at the bottom than the top (so it resembles the triangular form of a Christmas tree).

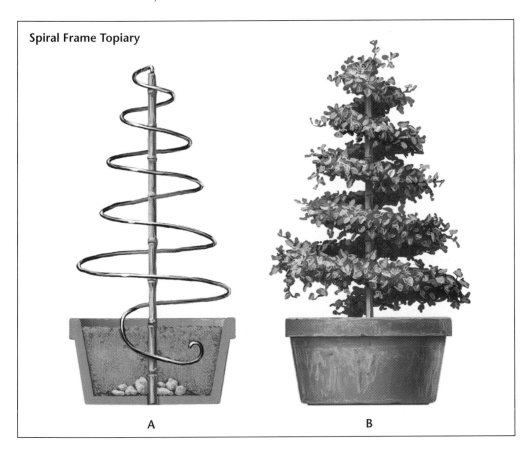

Spiral Frame Topiary

A   B

Step 3: Slip the wire around the stake and ram the top inch or so of wire into the stake's hollow end (see figure A on page 29). If it's loose, secure it with a bit of vinyl tape.

Step 4: Add some soil, and anchor the end to hold it steady. Plant an English ivy at the base and follow steps 5 and 6 for the tall circle on pages 24–25.

> **TIPS FOR SUCCESS**
>
> **GETTING BIG AND STUFFED**
>
> The leafy covering of a stuffed-frame topiary makes the finished sculpture appear much larger. For this reason you should plan and design your frame so that it's about an inch smaller all around than the size of the finished topiary you desire.

THE STUFFED-FRAME TOPIARY

The stuffed-frame topiary uses a form or frame shaped to a three-dimensional figure. Often, the frame is made of wire, but it might also be of a flexible wood like willow. Favorite shapes for stuffed-frame topiaries include an assortment of fanciful animals and birds, among them a beguiling array of bunnies, cats, turtles, swans, and dinosaurs. Wire frames exist for a goodly number of these creatures, but if you're ambitious, by all means create one yourself. This is where creative people can give free reign to their imagination (see Getting Wired on page 33).

The planting of a stuffed frame topiary is handled in various ways. One of the easiest techniques is the "up-and-around" method. In this approach, either a bushy upright species or several vining plants are trained to grow up and around the frame until it is completely covered.

A somewhat more demanding technique is the "moss-filled" method. In this approach, the frame itself is stuffed with sphagnum moss and a soilless mix and planted with very young plants or stem pieces called cuttings (these may be either cuttings that have already begun to grow roots or those that have not yet rooted). Eventually these plants will grow in the moss. Species favored for this purpose are usually the creepers or climbers that tolerate shallow growing conditions and root quickly (see Plants for Topiaries with Frames on page 37).

A STUFFED-FRAME BUNNY — THE UP-AND-AROUND METHOD

Step 1: Make or purchase a three-dimensional bunny frame. Partially fill a sturdy container with soil and anchor the frame securely to it (see figure A opposite).

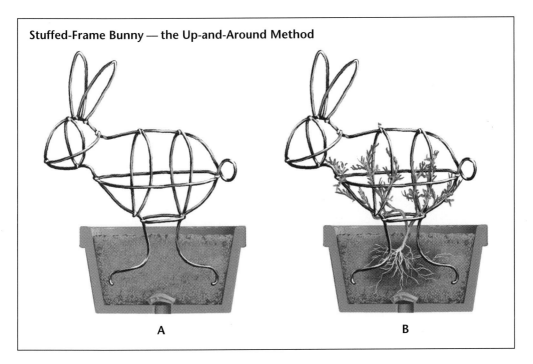

Stuffed-Frame Bunny — the Up-and-Around Method

A   B

Step 2: Select either a young, bushy upright plant (like rosemary or myrtle) or a vining or trailing species (like jasmine or English ivy). If your frame is less than a foot tall, choose a species with appropriately diminutive leaves. When leaves are too large, the topiary shape is obscured and its distinctive form gets lost.

Step 3: Position the plant in the soil close to the base of the frame and add sufficient soil to fill the container. Tamp the soil firmly to be sure that both plant and frame are securely in place.

Step 4: If you're using a shrubby plant, gently guide its main stem into the center of the frame (see figure B above). If you're using a vine, guide its stems up and around the frame as far as they will go. (With vines, if there's sufficient planting space in the container, you can use more than one plant.) Use twist-ties or raffia to secure to the frame as many twigs or stems as possible. Since the plants will probably be fairly young, don't be dismayed if only a few reach all sides of the frame at this time.

Step 5: For the next few months, water and fertilize the plants and encourage them to grow upward and outward around the form. As the stems lengthen, guide and bend them gently to cover as much of the frame as possible. Secure them as needed to keep them in place.

Step 6: Eventually, the frame will be completely covered. Continue to maintain a neat outline by pruning regularly, following the shape of the form.

A horse-shaped wire form is rapidly disappearing beneath its green cover of privet.

Getting Wired

You can find ready-made wire frames for topiaries at garden centers, specialty shops, and mail-order catalogs. If you're handy, you can make your own. This doesn't mean running to the nearest closet and grabbing an empty hanger — although a wire hanger is certainly useful for a simple diamond shape or square. However, it's better to visit your favorite hardware store for a roll of more workable material and some other useful supplies.

The wire that you're looking for must be supple and thin enough to bend easily, yet stiff enough to securely hold the topiary shape of your dreams. Dark aluminum wire, typically an 8 or 9 gauge, is the choice of many experts. Aluminum wire is both flexible and rustproof. It is also available encased in a thin plastic coating, which means it won't dirty your hands. (By the way, wire gauge numbers can be confusing at first because the sizes seem to go backward; this is because the *higher* the number the *thinner* the gauge.)

Also popular, and less expensive, is galvanized wire. Because it's stiffer, it's a bit harder to bend than aluminum. But this trait also makes it possible to use a thinner gauge, like 14 or 16, and know it will stay in shape. Like aluminum, galvanized wire won't rust, but it will eventually corrode. For this reason, many topiary-makers lacquer their finished frame. (Just remember to apply the coating before adding your plants.)

You may also wish to buy some chicken wire. Chicken wire is a practical way to form such geometric shapes as cones, spheres, or pyramids. A chicken wire "skin" can also convert a simple two-dimensional outline frame to a more elaborate three-dimensional design. Chicken wire is useful too for crumbling and stuffing into the open areas of large frames, and for a skin that keeps moss or plants in place. (Some topiary-makers find fishing line or nylon thread is also a useful skin.)

When you're finished perusing the wires, check the wire cutters. If you don't own one already, this is the time to choose a tool that is both comfortable to hold and easy to wield.

Also helpful when making frames is waterproof adhesive tape or the black material used by electricians. As you form the frame, the tape keeps the parts neatly fitted together and covers dangerous sharp edges.

Finally, there's the hot-glue gun. This is a strange gizmo, but most topiary-frame-makers swear by this clever tool. It dispenses a quick-drying glue to the joints of your frame; its instant seal ensures that the loose parts stay securely in place while you work and remain so until the frame is covered by plants.

A Stuffed-Frame Bunny — the Moss-Filled Method

Step 1: Make or purchase a three-dimensional bunny frame. If the frame does not stand securely by itself, anchor it to a simple support such as a flat platform to ensure that it remains firmly upright. Have on hand some chicken wire or nylon string (fishing line is a favorite) for use later to reduce the large spaces in the frame and give support where needed to the stuffing and plants (see figure A on page 35).

Step 2: Choose a trailing species to use, such as creeping fig *(Ficus pumila)* or baby's tears *(Soleirolia soleirolii)*. Buy small plants or make rooted cuttings of your selection, planning a minimum of five plants or cuttings per square foot or more if you're the impatient type. To determine the number of plants you'll need, approximate the square footage of the surface area (that's the height multiplied by the width for each side). Multiply that number by five, which will give you a reasonable number of plants per square foot you want. (To be sure that you don't run short, add 10 percent more plants.)

Step 3: Purchase enough sphagnum moss to fill the frame and soak it in water several hours at least, or overnight if possible. Your goal is a material that is soft and pliable enough to work with easily. Also have handy a bag or two of soilless potting mix.

Step 4: Beginning at the bottom, pack the frame densely with the damp moss up to a height of an inch or two (see figure B on page 35).

Step 5: Plant this portion by plunging the roots firmly into the moss (see figure C on page 35). If the roots are fragile or the moss does not easily yield, make a small hole (a pencil, chopstick, or thin screwdriver are useful tools for this).

Step 6: Add another inch or two of moss again, and then more plants. Where your framed creature is fairly rotund (usually around the middle), fill its hollow center with the soilless planting mix, taking care that it's covered with moss.

TIPS FOR SUCCESS

BUSHY IS BEST

Once a shaped or trained plant reaches the height or length you want, there is a secret for making it bushy and it has to do with the tip of the stem. This end point is called the apical bud. Special chemicals within this bud prevent the development of all buds beneath so this is the only portion that grows. Once it's removed, however — either by pruning with a shears or pinching with your fingernail — the growth-retarding substance is interrupted. This allows the side shoots, known as laterals, to grow. Repeating this process is what makes a plant bushy.

Stuffed-Frame Bunny — the Moss-Filled Method

A

B

C

D

Make Mine Ivy

Hate to wait? In a hurry for your topiary or espalier? Then use ivy. The advantage of these fast-growing creepers and climbers is that a bushy, elegant design is achieved with remarkable speed.

Although many kinds of creepers and climbers exist, the evergreen English ivy *(Hedera helix)* has proven itself especially satisfactory for creating topiaries with frames as well as espaliers on walls. In contrast with an apple tree or a boxwood—plants that take years to become impressive specimens—a work of English ivy can be a flourishing finished sculpture in just a few days.

Since ancient times, English ivy's distinctive form and its ability to survive both shade and drought have led to its popularity with gardeners. Along the way it has also achieved its place in myth and herbal lore. Among the more intriguing connections is an identification with Bacchus, the Roman god of wine, whose head is invariably encircled in an ivy wreath. In 1st-century Rome, ivy was recommended by herbalists as a preventative for drunkenness, although strangely enough, it was also recommended as a hangover cure. Ivy apparently was useful both coming and going. In any case, ivy's cocktail connections continued into the Middle Ages, when bunches of ivy or paintings of ivy were hung above tavern doors.

Ivy's seemingly countless variations of leaf tone and outline derive from its astonishing ability to suddenly produce new forms. So if you've ever worried about figuring out what hybrid is which, you will hardly be consoled to learn that at last count the American Ivy Society recognized some four hundred varieties. All presumably with distinctive leaf shapes, sizes, coloration, and rates of growth.

Even if you're a quick study, at just the point you think you're getting a handle on things, you'll discover that the matter is further complicated by the ivies' habit of developing different outlines as they mature. But never mind. Only the experts know for sure.

As you stroll through your favorite nursery, choose whatever form or shape appeals. When possible, select plants with long and vigorous shoots, and take the time to untangle them carefully when you begin. Despite ivy's reputation for attaching itself to its support, you'll find that it's up to you to tie the shoots so they grow securely on the frame. Once the stems reach the desired length, snip off the growing tips to inspire side branches and bushiness.

Many of the new cultivars and hybrids appear to be hardier than they were first given credit for. This means that if you grow your trained ivy plant outdoors, there's a good chance it will spring back to life from its base if a frost kills its upper parts. But since ivy topiaries are also such fine container plants, if you're in a frosty clime it's easy enough to avoid the loss of your treasured creation; just bring it indoors for winter.

Of the seemingly endless array of ivies in all shades and shapes, here are a few notables to look for:

Buttercup: Fast grower with yellow leaves that turn chartreuse in light shade

Deltoidea: Slow grower; also known as Sweetheart for its heart-shaped foliage

Duckfoot: Medium grower; sometimes called Oakleaf for its three-lobed leaves

Galaxy: Densely branching with narrow three-part leaves

Glacier: Rapid grower with gray-green leaves with silvery white edges

Gold dust: Densely variegated and easily grown

Itsy bitsy: Fast grower with dense branches and narrow, pointed leaves

Pedata: Fast grower with gray-green leaves and white veins

Where your framed creature is too thin for stuffing (usually at the extremities, like the feet, ears, or tail) use the longer stems of plants and cover the empty frame directly.

Step 7: Continue alternating moss stuffing and plants until the frame is completely filled and covered (see figure D on page 35). Then moisten your planted creature well by drenching it with a gentle spray of water.

Step 8: Continue keeping the topiary barely moist until the plants are well established, and then moisten it regularly as needed to keep the plants fit.

PLANTS FOR TOPIARIES WITH FRAMES

Here are some plants especially amenable to training on frames, either empty or stuffed. With the exception of the English ivy, none of the following are hardy outdoors in areas of severe frost.

Upright Plants
Fuchsia spp./ Fuchsia
Helicrysum angustifolium / Curry plant
Lantana montevidensis / Lantana
Plumbago capensis / Plumbago
Rosmarinus officinalis / Rosemary

Vines or Creepers
Bougainvillea glabra / Bougainvillaea
Cissus rhombifolia / Grape ivy
Ficus pumila / Creeping fig
Hedera helix / English ivy (see Make Mine Ivy
    on page 36)
Hoya carnosa / Wax plant
Jasminum spp. / Jasmine
Soleirolia soleirolii / Baby's tears

> **TIPS FOR SUCCESS**
>
> **RECORD THAT CUT**
>
> It's never too late to start that plant record you always wished you had. Just begin by removing and setting aside the nursery tags from each new species you've bought this year. Then, check existing plants and remove any tags that still remain. Tape these tags, one or two to a page, in a loose-leaf notebook, organized by season or year. As time goes by, add notes when the training or shearing begins, the speed of new growth after trimming, special fertilizers, pests encountered, or any other pertinent observations of use for the future.

Keeping Topiaries Tiptop

Keeping topiaries in tiptop shape is an ongoing project, but fortunately, a little care goes a long way.

First there's regular watering. The amount and frequency of watering needed will vary with the species (junipers can manage with less than bay), the season of the year (plants are thirstier when actively growing in spring than when slowing down in autumn), and the intensity of sun and heat (hotter usually means drier).

Container topiaries also benefit from monthly feedings. My favorite plant food is a diluted solution of fish emulsion, but any all-purpose, water-soluble houseplant fertilizer is useful. Remember that your goal is not to encourage quick growth, but to replace the soil nutrients as they're used and leached out of the soil.

Then, there are regular haircuts. You want to keep your plant bushy and dense, so it's better to snip with a fingernail or scissors every other week than attack it with a machete once a year. During these regular trimmings, take the time to look for dead twigs in the plant's center and occasionally thin some live stems there, too. This will allow sunlight and air to penetrate the interior of the plant and encourage the development of strong new shoots.

Keep an eye on the ties that bind. As the twigs mature and thicken, the twist-ties or raffia ties begin to tighten and the day will come when you must decide whether to loosen them, replace them, or get rid of them altogether if they no longer seem needed.

The day will come when your container topiary will need some cosmetic surgery — underground, that is — to keep it happy in its limited space. This is also known as root pruning and the thickness to be cut away can vary from a half inch up to several inches depending on the size of the container and how densely the roots are packed.

To root-prune your plant, simply lay it on its side and slide it out from its container (lay several sheets of newspaper first to keep your space clean). Then, with a sharp knife or pruning shears, sever several chunks of roots all around, or, if the roots are a solid mass, slice an inch or two from all sides.

Repot the plant in fresh soil, add a new stake if the old one has rotted and the plant is not self-supporting, and water well. Then, to compensate for the roots lost, give the top of the plant a good haircut, and your work for the day is done.

Only a Scrooge could resist the delightful whimsy of a leafy green mouse appropriately attired in bright blooms.

Coping with Creatures Indoors

White fly, aphids, mealybugs, scale, and other creepy creatures with equally creepy names are the bane of the gardener, especially indoors, and it's ever a mystery how such attacking hordes sneak in. Surely some arrive via hidden eggs on new plant purchases. Others undoubtedly arrive through an open window floating on the gentle breezes.

Whatever their mode of transportation, these unseen arrivals are definitely unwanted. However, there is fortunately a way of coping that's safe for you, children, and pets: zealous adhesion to sanitation. This is another way of saying *keep your plants clean.* The first line of defense is isolating new introductions until you're convinced they're squeaky clean and worthy of joining society.

An especially safe weapon in the indoor arsenal is fly paper. Hung close to the plant, it's not exactly beautiful to look at, but it does do the job with obvious flying invaders like white fly (and many other insects, most of which have at least one flying stage, even if you don't see it).

Less offensive visually, but equally nontoxic for flying pests, is the vacuum cleaner. In this case, the trick is to shake the plant lightly. When the marauders feel the movement, they'll fly away in a frenzy. That's your chance to snare them. A mothball added to the vacuum cleaner's bag ensures their quick demise.

Unfortunately, catching pests old enough to fly doesn't mean catching pests barely ready to hatch. For this, the method I like best is a regular soapy bath for every leafy member of the household.

Soap has long been an ally in the battle of the bugs, and in the 19th century, whale oil was a safe favorite for orchards. For reasons not fully understood, the ingredients in soap cause certain tissues to malfunction, and the insect dies. Some gardeners swear by the commercial insecticidal soaps sold at nurseries. But a reasonable substitute is any liquid soap used to hand-wash dishes. (Occasionally, sensitive plants are injured by strong soap solutions. Test several leaves a day ahead and watch for burned-looking tips or yellow or brown spotting.)

The bathing procedure itself is easy, especially for reasonably portable plants. First, fill your sink nearly full with warm water. Add several squirts of the soap, enough to work up a lather. Then cover the soil with a damp cloth, completely surrounding the stem. Holding the cloth in place with one hand, use the other to lift the pot. Dip the plant in *upside down* so that as many twigs and leaves as possible are submerged. Keep the plant under the sudsy solution for several seconds, then turn it so that all other twigs and leaves are also dunked. Some gardeners prefer to rinse their plants afterward with clear water, but I just let them drip dry, and I have never noticed a problem.

Potted plants too large or too heavy to turn upside down can be laid on their side at the edge of the sink (with the soil covered, as noted above) and their limbs gently bent and pushed beneath the water. For plants impossible to dunk, buy an insecticidal soap in a ready-to-spray container. I've found that a spray is not nearly as thorough as a dip, and sprays will make a mess of your floor. But they're a worthy alternative to doing nothing.

A soap treatment is most effective when administered on a regular basis: every month or so, and even weekly, through spring, when many nasty little beasts reproduce at alarming rates.

That being said, I will admit that sometimes even a Herculean effort won't work to control some pests. There comes a time in every gardener's life when the buggers do get control. When this happens, and the point of no return has arrived, I believe in being ruthless: *I eliminate the ailing plant.* I've found that a plant that's constantly under siege is not worth the effort required to try repeatedly to save it and then fail. It's important not to agonize. Get rid of it. A plant trained and shaped to a beautiful form should provide its owner only with pleasure, not pain.

TIPS FOR SUCCESS

TURN AND TURN AGAIN

Keep that windowsill topiary from growing lopsided. Plants tend to grow in one direction, bending and stretching toward the strongest light. To keep your indoor topiary growing evenly, turn the pot a quarter circle every other week and treat all sides to even exposure to the sun.

A wire candleholder is the moss-stuffed frame for a creeping fig (Ficus pumila) *that has half completed its ascent.*

CHAPTER 2
THE EXQUISITE ESPALIER

As a city slicker with no space to spare, I have long been intrigued by the espalier. These are exquisitely shaped plants — usually shrubs and small trees — that have been coerced into growing flat as pancakes so that their limbs form a single plane.

The word espalier (pronounced ess-PAL-yer) is believed to derive from a combination (or corruption) of the French word *epaule,* or shoulder, and the old Italian word *spalliera,* a kind of support. Whatever its origin, espalier is now used more or less interchangeably to refer to the plant that's been trained as well as to the training process itself.

The technique is thought to date from ancient Rome, where fruiting species were espaliered by farmers, whose goal was maximum yield in minimum space. Since the method also yields an unusually picturesque silhouette, nonfruiting espaliered plants are today exceedingly popular as ornamental objects in the landscape. Whether grown snug against a wall, fence, or lattice, or on a wire frame as a freestanding divider, espaliered shrubs and trees are delightfully decorative even as they are exceptionally practical where space is at a premium.

Early-summer white blooms add to the distinctive appeal of an espaliered Oriental dogwood (Cornus kousa).

STARTING YOUR ESPALIER

If you're endowed with an ample supply of patience and time and are a serious do-it-yourselfer, you certainly can make an espalier — it isn't nearly as difficult as it may seem.

First consider the various espalier shapes (see page 45) and choose a design that appeals. Below you will find directions for some of these outlines using specific plants. But if they're not the species you want, take a trip to your favorite nursery and buy the one you prefer (see Plants Amenable to Being Espaliered on page 58). Make sure that the specimen you choose is young enough to have a flexible stem and bendable limbs, and that it somewhat resembles the pattern you want.

If a fruiting tree is your goal, select a dwarfed or semi-dwarfed species. This will ensure that the mature specimen continues to fit comfortably in its allotted space. A full-size apple tree, for example, can quickly grow more than 25 feet, which makes for a rather unwieldy espalier.

TIPS FOR SUCCESS

STORE-BOUGHT ESPALIERS

It's not considered cheating if you start your espalier venture by purchasing a plant that's already been trained by a professional. Quite a few ornamental (that is, nonfruiting) espaliered plants, such as euonymus and yew, are available at reasonable cost. You'll find them in garden shops standing like stiff soldiers at attention, tied to their lattice wood frames. Pretrained fruiting plants are harder to come by. Since such plants typically take many more seasons to produce, when you do find one, it will likely be rather pricey.

FORMWORK FIRST

It is important to take time to prepare the formwork for your espalier. While it's possible to train an espalier directly on a solid fence or wall, some species — notably the fruiting ones or those vulnerable to mildews — are better off grown several inches away from the wall on wires or lattice. This small space permits air to circulate and helps control disease. It also makes pruning easier and repainting of the wall, if needed, possible.

To establish the espalier formwork, set two sturdy posts at the outermost spread of the space where you wish your plant to be. These posts should be as tall as the final espalier you prefer, a height that typically ranges from 2 to 7 feet high.

String between the posts three to five strands of heavy galvanized wire. Make them tight enough to support the espaliered limbs. Now you're ready to begin your design.

Espalier Shapes

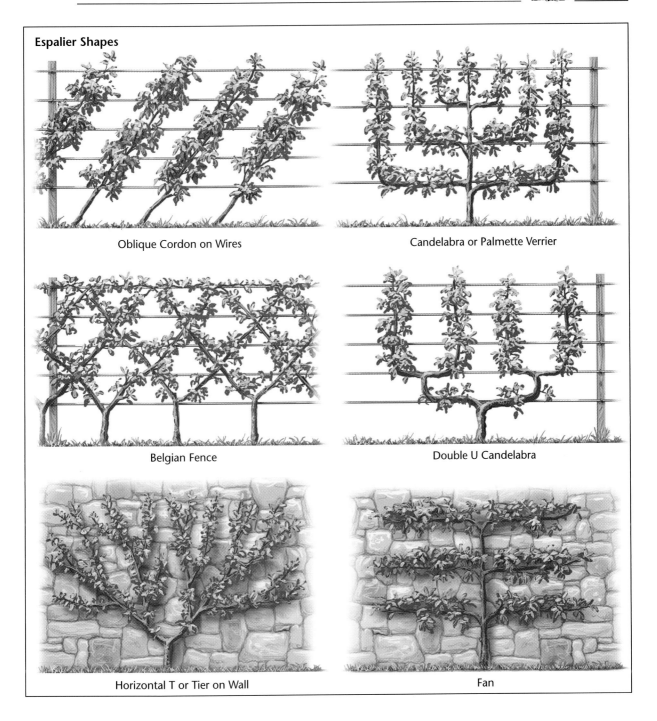

Oblique Cordon on Wires

Candelabra or Palmette Verrier

Belgian Fence

Double U Candelabra

Horizontal T or Tier on Wall

Fan

A DWARF-APPLE CORDON

One of the easiest, and certainly most versatile, espalier forms is the cordon. The word is French for cord or rope, but in espalier-speak it means a plant trained to grow in a single, slender line. (Those who prefer English call it the beanpole method.) A cordon espalier can be trained to grow in either a vertical, horizontal, or diagonal direction typically at 30°, 45°, or 60° angles. A vertical cordon of a fruiting species should be about 6 feet tall for good production. Although angled and horizontal fruiting cordons grow less vigorously than upright ones, they are generally more productive. This is because the sideward shape causes the plant's energy to be directed into the production of flowering and fruiting buds. Such buds are called spurs.

The directions that follow are for a single dwarf-apple (*Malus* spp.) cordon. But if you have space for an entire decorative wall, use the directions to grow several plants along the wire framework. Space them about 1½ feet apart.

Step 1: Secure to the framework a bamboo stick positioned at a 45° angle (see figure A on page 47).

Step 2: Next to the bamboo stake, plant a young, single-stemmed dwarf apple tree, making sure that the knob at the bottom of the stem is above the ground. This is the graft union with the roots.

> **TIPS FOR SUCCESS**
>
> **I GOT SPURS**
>
> Apples and pears are among the fruiting plants that produce flower buds and fruit on "spurs," which are actually stubby, modified limbs. When branches are trained horizontally, as is done with espaliers, the growth of these spurs is accelerated. Spurs on such fruiting trees as apples and pears live for many years. However, spurs on apricot trees die within two to five years, so their twigs must be pruned every other year to allow new fruit-producing limbs to develop. Other trees, such as peaches and nectarines, produce flowers and fruit on new shoots only, so they need pruning every year to ensure a continuous supply of new wood.

Step 3: Cut off all the side limbs near the stem, but leave four widely spaced buds. The single straight trunk that remains (known appropriately as a "whip") should then be secured to the angled bamboo support with twist-ties, raffia, or yarn (see figure B on page 47). Do not remove the growing tip (called a leader).

Step 4: The following spring, cut off any flowers that appear (see figure C on page 47). I know this is a heart-rending thing to do, but it's important as a means of preventing the early bearing of fruit. This gives the plant time to direct its energies into developing the espalier form.

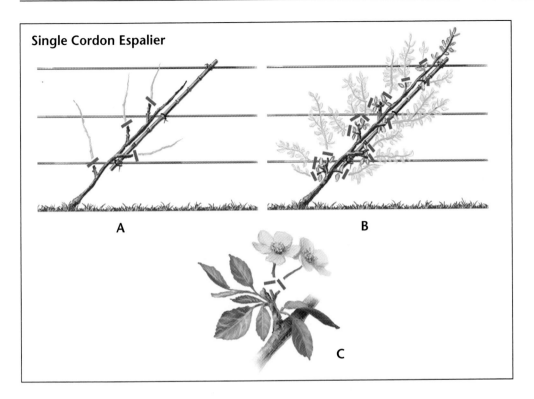

Single Cordon Espalier

A

B

C

Step 5: In late summer or early fall, cut back the side shoots, or laterals, to several good leaves and reduce the shoots that emerge to two buds. Do not remove the leader.

Step 6: Continue securing the leader as it grows and when it reaches the height you want, snip it off about 6 inches above the wire.

Step 7: Water the plant regularly and fertilize it following package directions for fertilizer concentrations. Continue to prune away new side shoots or stems.

Step 8: Within a few years, the plant will bear fruit and your cordon can be considered a success. To keep it healthy, periodically remove old stems to encourage fresh new fruiting shoots. If you wish, you can at this point remove the stakes and secure the plants directly to the wires. You can also now cut the leader back to an inch above the topmost wire.

A Belgian fence supported by bamboo stakes is a handsome garden divider as well as an airy backdrop for flowers.

A BELGIAN FENCE OF APPLES AND PEARS

A variation on the single cordon is the luxurious diamond grid or lattice form known as the Belgian fence. The simplest way is a series of overlapping diagonal cordons. One advantage of the cordon form of espalier is that several species of trees can be combined for a single design. So, if a wall of fruiting plants is your dream, combine cordons of apples and pears (or other compatible species).

Step 1: Secure to your wire framework for its entire length a series of bamboo sticks. Position them at 45° angles about 1¹⁄₂ feet apart.

Step 2: Next to each of the bamboo stakes, plant young, single-stemmed dwarf apple trees and pear trees. Alternate the two species. Make sure in each case that the knob of the root graft union is above ground.

Step 3: Follow the cordon steps 3 to 7 as directed on pages 46–47. In a few years the plants should mature sufficiently to bear fruit and simultaneously provide you with a most decorative wall or space divider.

Belgian Fence Espalier: Alternative Method (Using Two Shoots)

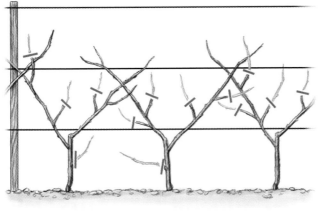

First year

Plant young, single-stemmed trees about 2 feet apart beneath a sturdy wire trellis. Cut them back to about 18 inches, then select two shoots to train at a 45° angle and trim as shown.

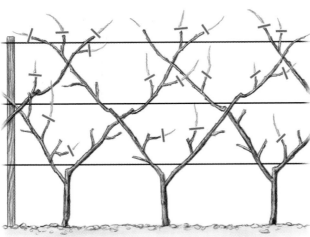

Second and subsequent years

Late winter is best for pruning. Train emerging twigs as shown and snip the tops when the plant reaches the height you desire.

A PEAR TIER OR HORIZONTAL T

After the cordon, the tier or horizontal T is the most easily created espalier form. This outline consists of a central stem from which the horizontal tiers or arms grow at intervals along the wire frame. A minimum of four wires is best for a handsome design.

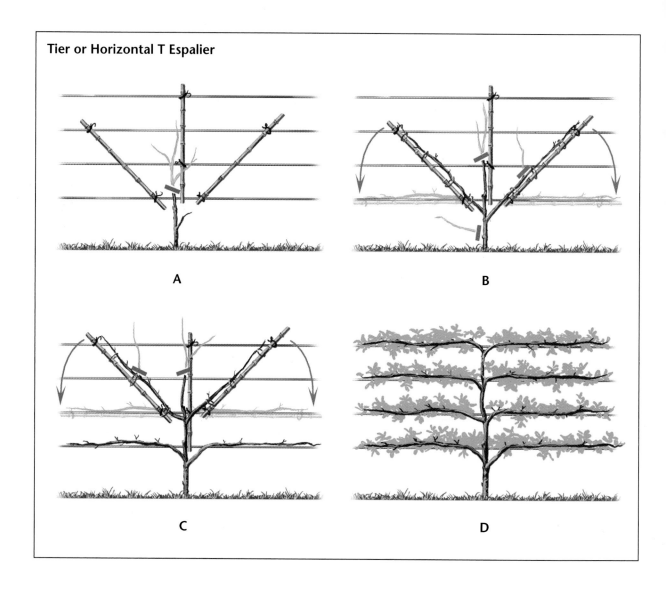

Tier or Horizontal T Espalier

A

B

C

D

Step 1: Begin your tier or horizontal T by planting a young, flexible-limbed pear tree *(Pyrus communis)* at the center point of your supporting frame.

Step 2: Trim the leader to the height of the first horizontal line on the frame, leaving at least three small branches, or buds, below the cut (see figure A).

Step 3: Position an upright bamboo stick directly above the leader and secure it to your wire form. Position two other sticks at 45° angles outward from the plant (see figure A).

Step 4: Allow the topmost bud to develop and grow upward, securing it as it lengthens to the upright bamboo stick. Allow two vigorous growing shoots from the lower buds to develop. As they lengthen, tie them to the two side bamboo supports. Remove all other twigs.

Step 5: At summer's end, gently bend the bamboo sticks down to the lowest wire of your frame and tie it carefully to the support (see figure B).

Step 6: When the leader reaches the next horizontal wire, repeat the process to create a second tier (see figure C).

Step 7: Continue yearly for as long as it takes to reach the number of horizontal wires you have on your form (see figure D).

TIPS FOR SUCCESS

FIREBLIGHT

A nasty bacterial disease known as fireblight affects such members of the rose family as apple, pear, pyracantha, and cotoneaster. Fireblight was first recorded in America in the late 18th century, and the name is an apt description of the blackened flowers, leaves, and twigs, which do indeed look burned by fire. The bacteria overwinters on branches on sunken lesions called cankers and oozes out in spring. It is then spread by wind, rain, and insects to new areas. By midsummer there may be extreme branch and twig dieback.

To control fireblight, cut off and destroy infected twigs at least a foot below the afflicted portion. After pruning, sterilize your shears in a mix of water and bleach. Do not feed infected plants with high nitrogen fertilizers since these force a rapid growth of shoots and suckers that are especially vulnerable to the disease. You can also try preventing the disease by spraying with copper sulfate in early spring.

A simple U-shaped espalier gives a rustic shingle wall a textured green accent.

A QUINCE CANDELABRA

Another formal and most elegant espalier is the candelabra, whose proper French name is *palmette verrier,* a term honoring Louis Verrier, a 19th-century French teacher, head gardener at an agricultural school, and master of espalier artistry. A variation on the candelabra shape is a two-branched form, or a double U (see page 45).

Espaliered pear trees are decorative as well as unusually reliable, producing a regular crop of fruit as seen on this symmetrical planting of two candelabras.

Step 1: Secure to the wire framework seven tall bamboo sticks that you have sunk several inches into the ground (see figure A on page 55).

Step 2: Next to the bamboo stake in the center, plant a young, single-stemmed quince tree *(Cydonia oblonga)*. Cut it back to just below the lowest wire on your frame (figure A), leaving several small shoots.

Step 3: Allow three vigorous shoots to develop into small stems. Secure the center stem to the closest bamboo stake and gently bend the other two stems outward in opposite directions. Tie them to the lowest horizontal wire on your frame (figure B).

Step 4: Allow the center stem to grow upward until it reaches the next horizontal wire and cut it just below that line.

Step 5: Allow three more shoots to develop on the leader and secure it to the closest stake. Gently bend the other two stems outward and tie them to the second horizontal wire (figure C).

Step 6: When the lowest tier of horizontal stems reaches the outermost stakes, bend the stems gently upward and tie them securely. Do the same with the second tier (figure C).

Step 7: Repeat steps 5 and 6 until all stakes are covered and the vertical arms reach the topmost wire. Then cut these stems at that level (figure D).

Step 8: Continue to water and fertilize. Prune regularly to maintain the candelabra outline. In a few years, if you wish, remove the wood stakes and secure the limbs directly to the wire form.

Candelabra Espalier

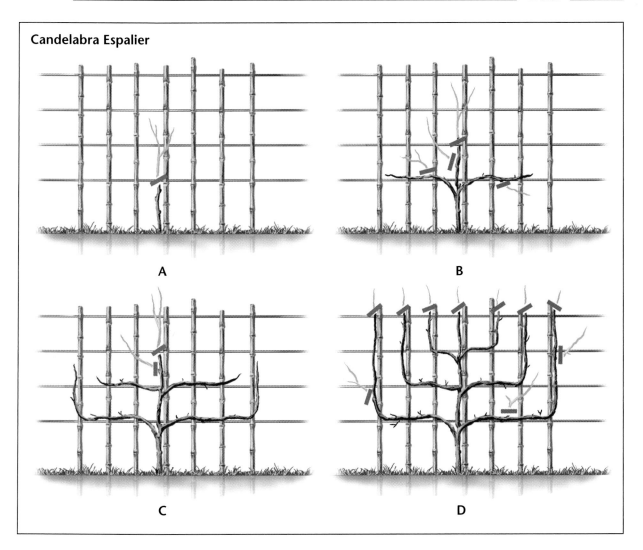

A

B

C

D

When making a candelabra espalier, some gardeners prefer to position the wire framework close to a wall that needs decorating. After the candelabra is formed, both stakes and wires can be removed and the espaliered plant secured directly to the wall if continued support is needed. Some trees, however — and the quince is one of them — are strong enough when mature to stand alone. Often, no further support is needed.

A PEACH FAN

And finally, there is the V-shaped espalier or fan. An advantage to this outline is its flexibility. Plants can be maintained in a strictly formal shape or in a much more relaxed shape. For this reason, it is a useful method for shrubs and trees whose limbs are not so flexible that they bend easily. A formal V, with branches radiating upward from two arms, is a favorite for fruiting species.

Step 1: Plant at the center of your supporting wire framework a young peach tree *(Prunus persica)* and cut it back to about 2 feet above the ground, or the

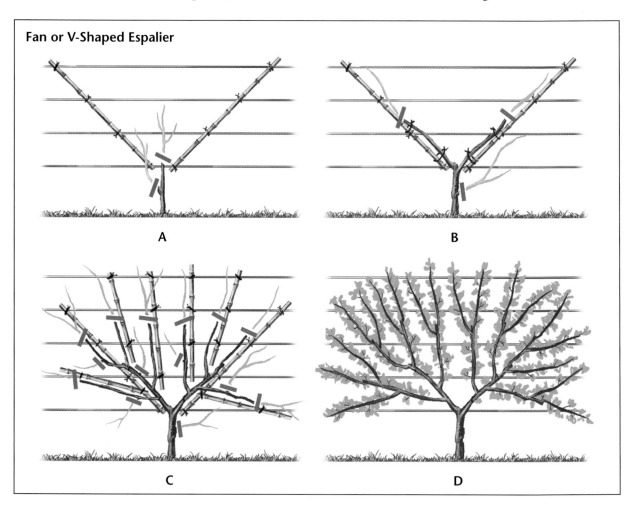

Fan or V-Shaped Espalier

A

B

C

D

A simple fan is an easily achieved espalier shape.

height of your first line of wire. Make sure there are several buds below the cut (see figure A on page 56).

Step 2: Secure to the wire two bamboo sticks positioned at 45° angles. These are for future branch support.

Step 3: The following spring, tie to the bamboo supports two of the most vigorous side shoots (see figure B on page 56) and after you see these are growing well, eliminate all the other horizontals. Let these two main shoots develop and secure them as they lengthen.

Step 4: The next growing season, choose four sturdy stems on each limb and tie them to additional supporting stakes (see figure C on page 56). If possible, try to locate two on the upper side of each branch, the third on the bottom, and the fourth at the end. Once these are growing well, remove all the others.

Step 5: The following winter, cut the branches back by a third.

Step 6: The next year choose the four best stems as before and remove the rest. Continue yearly, allowing new shoots to develop at 3- or 4-inch intervals along the frame and pinching the tips in late summer, or until the fan reaches the limits of its allotted space (see figure D on page 56).

PLANTS AMENABLE TO BEING ESPALIERED

Although the steps just outlined are for creating espaliers of specific fruiting plants, you can apply the same general principles and train nonfruiting plants, which are also known as ornamental species. Here is a selection of the many shrubs and small trees, both fruiting and ornamental, that are particularly amenable to the bending and pruning required in the espaliering process.

Citrus spp. / Orange, lime, lemon
Sun
Zone 10
Tropical citrus fruit trees and shrubs are remarkable for their versatility when it comes to accepting a shape. Most have handsome shiny foliage with fragrant small white blooms and a cheerful adaptability to container life. Louis IV (a cold-climate gardener) had his grown in tubs by the hundreds and moved them indoors for the winter.

Euonymus alata / Winged burning bush
Sun or part shade
Zone 3
The peculiar corky growths that line its stems give this plant its winged appearance, and its vivid autumn crimson does indeed make it look like it's on fire.

Steel and wire are the sturdy supports for this mature crabapple espalier.

An exquisitely trained crabapple offers the added attraction of a decorative diagonal lattice and white board backdrop.

Informal espaliers like this firethorn are quick and simple beautifiers for any vertical surface.

When left uncut this slow growing, versatile shrub eventually reaches about 15 feet in height and spread. 'Compacta' is shorter, denser, and more upright in form.

Malus spp. / Apple and crabapple
Sun or part shade
Zones vary

A seemingly infinite number of apple and flowering crabapples exist to brighten the garden. A traditional favorite for espaliers in medieval monastery gardens, these delightful plants are equally at home on a modern city rooftop or backyard. Look for the knob at the base of the trunk, which indicates a graft, and plant it well above the soil line. Flower colors range from deep magenta through white. To get the color you want, purchase in spring when the plants are in bloom.

Nerium oleander / Oleander
Sun or light shade
Zone 10

The good news is that this shrubby small tree, which can reach at least 20 feet tall, is a stunner when covered with its 2-inch-wide elegant pink, red, white, or purple flowers. The bad news is that all parts are poisonous if ingested. If you have no young children to worry about, by all means try the many easily grown cultivars, including dwarf forms like 'Petite Pink', which rarely exceeds 3 to 5 feet. 'Algiers', which has dark red blooms and grows to about 6 feet tall, has narrow leaves that are dark green above and pale underneath.

Taxus spp./ Yew
Sun and part or full shade
Zones vary
This slow-growing evergreen, with its lustrous flat dark green needles, manages to withstand an extraordinary range of trying soil and light conditions. The Japanese yew *(Taxus cuspidata),* hardy to Zone 4, includes many upright or spreading forms. *T.c.* 'Capitata' can reach a height of about 40 feet and turns bronze in winter, and 'Nana' is a slow grower that usually remains short and fat. Less hardy is the English yew *(T. baccata)*. One of its elegant offspring is the Irish yew *(T.b.* 'Stricta'), which has unusually dark green needles.

ADDITIONAL PLANTS TO ESPALIER

Fruiting Plants

Zone 5	*Cydonia oblonga* / Fruiting quince
	Prunus avium / Sweet cherry
	Pyrus communis / Pear
Zone 6	*Prunus persica* / Peach
	Prunus persica / Nectarine
Zone 8	*Punica granatum* / Pomegranate
Zone 10	*Fortunella margarita* / Kumquat

A stone building is a superb textured backdrop for an espaliered yew.

A blank wall is skillfully decorated by bougainvillea trained on diagonal wires.

Ornamentals

Zone 5	*Euonymus fortunei* / Wintercreeper	
Zone 6	*Euonymus japonica* / Japanese spindle tree	
	Ilex crenata / Japanese holly	
	Pyracantha coccinea / Firethorn	
Zone 7	*Camellia japonica* / Camellia	
	Magnolia grandiflora / Southern magnolia	
	Podocarpus macrophyllus / Yew pine	
	Rosmarinus officinalis / Rosemary	
Zone 9	*Hibiscus rosa-sinensis* / Hibiscus	
Zone 10	*Nerium oleander* / Oleander	

The glowing berried limbs of an espaliered firethorn 'Mohave' add an orange rhythm to fall.

Alternative Method of Grape Training

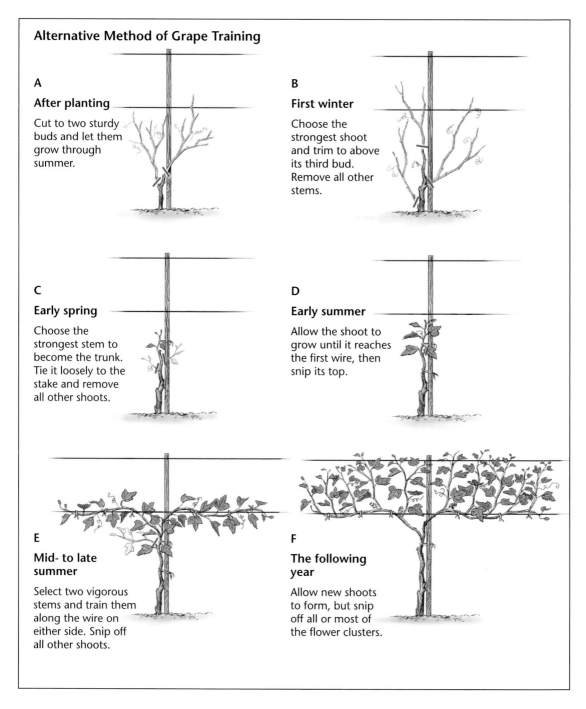

A

After planting

Cut to two sturdy buds and let them grow through summer.

B

First winter

Choose the strongest shoot and trim to above its third bud. Remove all other stems.

C

Early spring

Choose the strongest stem to become the trunk. Tie it loosely to the stake and remove all other shoots.

D

Early summer

Allow the shoot to grow until it reaches the first wire, then snip its top.

E

Mid- to late summer

Select two vigorous stems and train them along the wire on either side. Snip off all other shoots.

F

The following year

Allow new shoots to form, but snip off all or most of the flower clusters.

ESPALIERED VINES AND CLIMBERS

As I drove through a Portuguese vineyard not long ago, I was reminded that fruiting shrubs and trees were not the only crop plants historically trained as espaliers. The grape was too, and for the same reason: maximum yield in minimum space. Even if wine-making is not high on your list of chosen activities, you can be sure that grapes lend themselves quite well to decorative espaliering. This is one of the easiest of the various methods to use.

AN EASY GRAPE ESPALIER

Step 1: Secure to the center of your wire framework a single sturdy bamboo stick and plant your grape vine *(Vitis vinifera)* next to it.

Step 2: Pick the strongest stem for the main trunk and secure it to the bamboo.

Step 3: When the main trunk reaches the top wire, cut it off. Also cut away all other stems (properly known as canes), leaving two vigorous buds or shoots at each level of your wire form.

Step 4: Allow these side buds to develop into canes and secure them to the wires forming outward facing arms at each level of wire. Cut away all other stems.

Step 5: Permit these outward-heading canes to grow sufficiently to produce about 10 buds each, and then cut their growing tip. These will be your fruit bearing canes for the current year.

Step 6: Remove all other canes except for four other vigorous shoots. Cut these back to about two buds. These will be your bearing canes for the next year.

Step 7: Continue watering and fertilizing the plants. Early each spring, remove the 10-bud canes of the previous year. This will ensure the production of the fresh young wood on which the fruit is produced.

OTHER KINDS OF VINES AND CLIMBERS TO ESPALIER

In addition to grapes, many other vining or climbing plants may be trained as an espalier. Keep your pruners ready: the controlled outline is hardly a natural form for climbing types that prefer to ramble at will. To keep your decorative vine in firm espalier control, you'll have to pay regular attention to it. This is a list of plants to consider.

Actinidia delicosa / Kiwi or Chinese gooseberry

Actinidia polygama / Hardy kiwi

Bougainvillaea glabra / Bougainvillea

Ficus pumila / Creeping fig

Hedera helix hybrids / English ivy hybrids (see Make Mine Ivy on page 36)

Hydrangea petiolaris / Climbing hydrangea

Passiflora edulis / Passion fruit

Parthenosissus tricuspidata / Boston ivy

Rosa spp. / Climbing roses

A two-story espalier is a tracery of white in the snow.

Chapter 3
Tied in Knots

My first close look at a home-grown patterned landscape, as opposed to one in a public garden, took place among the bricks and concrete of Manhattan. Hidden behind a brownstone was a simple, but elegant, tracery of boxwood. Despite limited space — the entire garden measured maybe 20 feet by 28 — that gardener had created a superb green design for his upstairs window view. And a delightful sight it was.

The patterned landscape, as the array of knots, parterres, mazes, and other similar designs are sometimes called, has existed in one form or another for many centuries. The earliest designs, often fashioned of low stones or turf, are believed to have been mazes or labyrinths inspired by Greek mythology and pagan ritual. Although these early shapes may have had a magical or religious purpose (a symbol of the journey through life, some believe), garden patterns of hedge plants have served as purely decorative and even quite playful garden features since the Renaissance.

Silvery lavender cotton (Santolina chamaecyparissus) *and green germander* (Teucrium chamaedrys) *combine nicely for color and texture contrast in a small knot.*

It takes only four curved lines within boxwood squares to create a seemingly complex pattern in the herb garden at the New York Botanical Garden.

The knot garden is thought to have its origins in the Middle Ages, when monks in monasteries carved geometric four-part beds for medicinal and culinary herbs. By the 15th century, a square of low hedges with additional plants intricately crossed and intertwined had become a garden favorite in England. Although presently popular as an outline for herbs, in these early designs the separate beds were filled with colored gravel, sand, chalk, or coal.

In 17th-century France, another group of patterns evolved featuring intricate and ever more fluid patterns. These complex, free-flowing scrolls, arabesques, and fleurs-de-lis were called *parterres,* the French word for "on the ground." A more elaborate form, the *parterre-en-broderie,* enhanced with flowers, was inspired by the embroidered fashions of the day.

A BOXWOOD KNOT

Your plans for your garden may not include such expansive or elaborate compositions, but you can certainly learn from these historic forms and borrow useful elements for a patterned landscape of your own. In fact, it isn't at all difficult to create a simple knot of dwarf boxwood (*Buxus sempervirens* 'Suffruticosa') in less space than most people suspect.

Step 1: First, decide where your knot should be located (it should be in a spot with as much sun as possible) and how large a design is appropriate for your site. Keep in mind that bigger is not necessarily better, and a simple and most manageable knot can be created in a space no greater than 10 by 10 feet. The one I made in my mid-Manhattan garden is a mere 6 by 6 feet.

Step 2: Once you've established a comfortable size, mark on the ground the outer limits of the square shape of your knot. You can do this by dragging a spade or shovel across the soil, or, as one of my more inventive gardening friends did, by using a can of spray paint and drawing right on the earth. To get the lines

> **TIPS FOR SUCCESS**
>
> **CARPET BEDDING**
>
> Near the end of the 18th century, an influx of what was then considered exotic tropical plants arrived in Great Britain from the far corners of the colonies. This led to the colorful summer arrangements called carpet bedding. A kind of high Victorian variation on the classic French *parterre,* these garden displays consisted of mostly low growing flowering species or plants with colorful leaves, massed in showy, sometimes garish patterns. Set in an open stretch of lawn, most carpet beds traced simple circles or curves, while a few took such fanciful forms as a floral clock or the homeowner's initials. Carpet bedding continues to remain especially popular in America as a landscape feature on the grounds of suburban corporate headquarters.

straight, hammer a temporary stake into the ground at the edge of each corner and run a string between them as a guide (see figure A below).

Step 3: Bisect this square with two additional lines for a simple but elegant form. You can do this either with two diagonal lines, which creates a pattern composed of four triangular beds (see figure B below), or with one horizontal and one vertical line, which creates a pattern composed of four rectangular beds (see figure C below). You now have the locations for the plantings that form the knot.

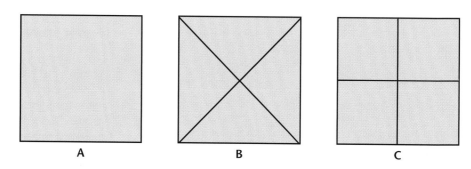

A   B   C

Step 4: A little math comes next to determine how many plants you will need. To do this, first measure and note the number of linear feet of the square you have outlined on the ground. Then measure and note the two additional lines you have drawn. Add these figures together for your total linear feet. Multiply that final figure by two to get the number of plants you'll need. This figure is based on the assumption you will use two plants per linear foot (which means plants spaced about 6 inches apart).

The actual number will depend on the size of the plants you find in your nursery and the amount you wish to spend. Bushier plants will cost more, but you won't need as many; skimpy plants are less expensive, but it will take longer for the pattern to form. If your budget is tight, plan on purchasing one plant per linear foot, and then add an extra plant for each line of pattern (which, in this design, will be six). The best plants to purchase are those in plastic nursery containers or with their roots wrapped in burlap and not bare-root plants (see Buying Hedge Plants on page 88).

Golden-leaved euonymus adds bright contrast to this boxwood pattern.

Step 5: Place your newly purchased plants at regular intervals along the lines you've drawn on the ground. Look to see whether the pattern you've created is the one you want. This is when the use of container-grown nursery stock is especially practical. Plants in pots are most easily moved and can be rearranged without damage.

Step 6: Once it's clear that your chosen plants fit comfortably in a pattern that works, dig the holes or trenches and plop them in (see Planting the Plants on page 88).

Step 7: Water the plants well. Clip to start the neat hedge outline. Later, the spaces between can be filled colored mulches, flowers, or herbs, and the center embellished with an elegant bit of architecture — a sundial, perhaps, or a fountain or statue.

Easy Knot Variations

After your basic knot shape is in place with the potted plants (step 5), you may discover you have the space and inclination and wish to create a variation of the basic form. This is your chance to change your design. The drawing on page 77 shows just some of the variations possible. At the center of my knot garden, for example, I eliminated the crossed diagonal lines of plants and replaced it with a circle.

Another simple shape can be created with a second square in the center or with another crossing lines.

The variations of outline are numerous. If, for example, a square knot does not appeal or perhaps doesn't fit your space, use a rectangular variation. Knots can also be created with intertwining, weaving, or curving lines of plants. Use a flexible hose to help you trace this outline.

The plants you choose can also make your knot pattern more interesting, especially if you combine plants with different leaf shapes or tones. With your outline of boxwood in place, for example, you might make the center legs of lavender *(Lavandula angustifolia)* or germander *(Teucrium chamaedrys)*. Or you could combine two species of lavender cotton, the silver-gray leaved *Santolina chamaecyparissus* and the green-leaved *S. virens*.

Plants for Knots

Species with smaller leaves or a fine texture are often the ideal scale for use in the small patterned landscape. To keep your pattern clean and neat, combine no

Basic Knot Variations

more than two or three species. Here are some plants to consider for knots, parterres, mazes, and other patterned landscapes.

Buxus sempervirens / Boxwood
Sun or light shade
Zone 6

For folks like me, who adore its fragrance, there's nothing like a waft of boxwood on a sunny summer day. In existence since the days of ancient Rome, these elegant, long-lived plants grow best in moist, well-drained soil. The many hybrids are descended primarily from two species: *B. microphylla,* the Japanese or little-leaf box, and *B. sempervirens,* the common English or American box. Hardiness varies with the countless cultivars, but success is more likely if you purchase from a reliable local nursery, preferably one a few miles north of where you garden. New and reputedly tough hybrids include 'Green Velvet', which grows to form a 3-foot mound, and 'Green Gem', which rarely exceeds 2 feet. In frosty areas, do your boxwood planting in spring.

Lavandula angustifolia / Lavender
Sun
Zone 6

Another plant whose heady scent I adore, lavender, alas, hates my too-shady site. Full sun is a must for the many species and varieties. Aromatic, gray-green foliage covers these bushy plants, which grow between 1 and 3 feet high and produce their distinctive pale purple flower spikes through summer. *L. angustifolia* 'Munstead' is a light purple early bloomer, while *L.a.* 'Hidcote' is dark. Less hardy is the French lavender *L. dentata candicans,* which is distinguished by finely cut, somewhat ferny-looking foliage. The lavenders thrive with minimal moisture.

Santolina chamaecyparissus and *S. virens* / Lavender cotton
Sun
Zone 6

Do be sure to save the leaves clipped from lavender cotton for your closet, for they reputedly help repel moths. But even if they didn't, you'd enjoy their aromatic presence and marvelous color contrast in the garden. *S. chamaecyparissus* is

The Amazing Maze

A maze needs more room than a knot (although I don't suggest taking as much space as the one created in England that covered six acres and was made of corn). Obviously, the more space, the better for maze divider hedges are usually taller than those used for knots to hide the person walking through them. However, I recently saw a small children's maze in Florida that used low plants.

In any case, the steps for planning and planting a maze are similar to those used for the knot. You can create a small and relatively simple maze with a basic shape consisting of four concentric squares or rectangles.

Establish these outlines first (follow knot steps 1 through 5 on pages 73–75) and then locate the openings and the blind ends right in the field. If you don't trust your eye, plan the tricks of the maze on a piece of cardboard first. (Cardboard is better than paper since once outside, it's easy to hold securely and won't flap in the wind.) As with the knot, test your plan first by moving the plants about; then you can do the planting.

Three concentric rectangles of precisely clipped boxwood create a classic mazelike pattern.

Swirls and curves of boxwood organize the pattern in a colorful floral landscape.

Clumps of newly planted green and gray lavender cotton hint at the final shape of a pattern composed of circles and squares.

Free Potpourri

So you're outside clipping and shaping your plants, enveloped in the heady aroma of scented geraniums and santolina. Stop. Don't throw those clippings away. Scoop them up and save them for use in your own fragrant blend. It's easy to make yourself. And best of all, it's free.

Despite what you may think when you see a packet of potpourri in a fancy boutique, there's nothing mysterious about making it. It's as easy as drying fragrant leaves, drying colorful flowers, and then mixing them together. The secret to success lies in making sure that all the plant parts used are absolutely dry before they're blended.

Save for potpourri the leaves and small stems from such species as rosemary, lavender, santolina, lemon verbena, lemon balm, box, and bay. Superb too are any and all of the scented geraniums (among them, apple, rose, and peppermint). I also harvest whatever colorful garden flowers are currently in bloom (like rose, calendula, anemone, gomphrena, monarda, lilies, and salvia). Do your snipping early in the day, after the dew has dried. If I'm short on color, I add petals from a store-bought bouquet.

Spread these bits and pieces on a screen or cookie sheet lined with paper towels. Place them in a well-ventilated spot away from the sun and leave them for several days. (If they're soggy, the paper towels should be changed at least once.) Stir them daily to be sure that all the pieces are exposed to the air. Depending on the room temperature and humidity, everything should be dry and ready to use within a week. But beware. If you use the leaves or petals before they're *fully* dry, they'll mold and rot, and your potpourri will be ruined.

What's a good recipe for potpourri? It is generally best to have one fragrance predominate. A favorite is rose petals — about a quart — blended with a quart of two or three other fragrant leaves or petals for a secondary scent. Actually, any pleasing combination of colorful petals and fragrant leaves will do, for there are no rules. Don't be afraid to experiment. And do use your imagination.

To heighten the aroma of your blend, add to each quart of dried leaves and flowers a single drop of perfumed essential oil. Tiny bottles of these oils — in choices that include not only rose, but lavender, lily-of-the-valley, and jasmine — are available at herbal pharmacies or nurseries that specialize in herbs. Some gardeners also add a spoon of one or more pungent spices, such as cinnamon, allspice, cloves, or nutmeg, which are delightful in autumn and through the winter holidays. Another favorite is a spoon or two of the peel of dried orange, tangerine, or lemon.

After the oil and spices are added and the dried ingredients mixed, it's important to add a fixative to ensure the longevity of your fragrance. The best is orris root, which comes from the Florentine iris *I. pallida* and is available in powdered form. One tablespoon per quart of petals will suffice. It is sold at herb nurseries and special pharmacies.

All that's left to do is stir the blend, pour the potpourri in a decorative bowl, and sniff it whenever you walk by. When you'd like to give someone a special gift, fill an attractive, sparkling jelly jar with your potpourri, attach a decorative label, and add a colorful bow. Your home-grown offering is ready.

silvery gray, *S. virens* is green. If left untrimmed through late spring, the finely cut leaves will be dotted with bright yellow flowers in summer. These are rapid growers that can reach 3 feet in height as well as width. They shrug off drought, heat, and poor soil.

ADDITIONAL PLANTS FOR KNOTS

Zone 4   *Euonymus alatus* 'Compactus' / Dwarf euonymus
              Pinus mugo mugo / Mugo pine
              Taxus media 'Hicksii' and *T. cuspidata* 'Nana' / Yew

Zone 5   *Teucrium chamaedrys* / Germander

Zone 6   *Cotoneaster microphyllus* / Cotoneaster
              Ilex crenata 'Compacta' / Japanese holly

Zone 7   *Helicrysum angustifolium* / Curry plant

Zone 8   *Myrtus communis* / Myrtle
              Podocarpus macrophyllus / Yew pine
              Rosmarinus officinalis / Rosemary

CHAPTER 4

HEDGING YOUR BETS

ood hedges make good neighbors — maybe even better than fences (with
apologies to Robert Frost). Lofty hedgerows were used in the Middle Ages
to define property and contain domestic animals. Small hedge plants were used
in monastaries to divide medicinal and culinary herbs.

Later, in Versailles, that great 17th-century French garden, artfully shaped
hedges, trimmed by an army of gardeners, gave an elegant architectural feel to
the outdoor rooms of the Sun King's vast landscape.

HEDGES AS DECORATION

Continuing in this tradition, hedges remain an important decorative landscape
element. Clipped tight and small, they are the ornate knot for a central feature
or an artistic border for annuals and herbs. Clipped tight and tall, they are the

Low hedges sheared in a precise zigzag
pattern complement a wall-trained
arch, creating architectural interest in
a narrow space.

A tall hedge hides a charming garden with a wagon-wheel knot.

elegant backdrop for perennials and shrubs or the beautifying cover for unsightly views. Tall hedges are also a delightful way of tempering the wind or muffling the sound of traffic. In the modern garden, a handsome hedge can provide the privacy that helps ensure sanity. It is the ultimate in decorative screens for neighbors and passersby.

Symmetrically shaped hedges with large triangular caps provide privacy as well as distinction to a streetside entrance.

Buying Hedge Plants

For a good fast start — whether your hedge is planned as a fanciful knot or an elegant backdrop — it's essential to begin with healthy, well-developed, and well-branched plants with a generous set of established roots. The best way to do this is to buy plants grown in nursery containers or the ones called B&B (which means plants whose ball of roots is surrounded by soil and wrapped in burlap). Unless your budget is very tight, avoid those spindly bargains known as bare-root plants — which perfectly describes their condition.

Container or B&B plants are more expensive, it's true — but they're also a classic example of the buyer getting what he or she pays for. They're easier to plant successfully and are usually sturdy enough so they won't wilt and die if you forget to water in those important first weeks. You can move them around until you get the design you want, and, best of all, the hedge of your dreams will be a reality sooner.

In an ideal world, planting would take place as soon as possible after a nursery visit. But because this rarely happens, take the time to store unplanted new purchases in a wind-sheltered spot, preferably in bright, dappled sunlight, and keep the roots barely moist until they're safe in the ground.

Planting the Plants

Prepare for planting by digging either a trench or a line of holes. A garden hose is a useful linear guide if you want to establish a straight line. For more precision, hammer a temporary stake into the ground at each end and run a string between the stakes as a guide. If the purpose of your hedges is to edge your property, plant well within your side of the boundary. As your green screen matures and spreads, a cantankerous neighbor has the right — legitimately — to chop off leafy intruders. A staggered double row is best for hedges planned for use as a windbreak.

If you're a rooftop or terrace gardener, organize your containers before you get your plants. In regions subject to frost, a safe minimum tub size for winter

A towering evergreen hedge is the stylish backdrop for a formal herb garden where low hedges outline the beds.

protection is 18 inches deep and wide. Prepare for planting by filling them partway with a blend of equal amounts of topsoil, perlite, and compost or peat moss.

How far apart should your hedge plants be planted? The answer depends on the species' rate of growth, their ultimate size, and how quickly you want to see results. Plants for a decorative divider that's to be 6 feet tall or higher are usually spaced between 18 and 24 inches apart. Plants for a border backdrop that's to be 4 feet high can be 12 to 18 inches apart. Plants for a knot garden hedge planned to be 2 feet high or less can be 6 to 12 inches apart. The farther apart the hedges are, the longer it takes for the hedge shape to form.

Before planting, prepare the soil well by stirring into the area a shovelful of well-rotted manure along with several handfuls of a granular 5-10-5 fertilizer. After planting, form a shallow depression around each plant to catch rain and direct it to the roots. Then water well.

An arched passage is carved through a glorious hedge of beeches.

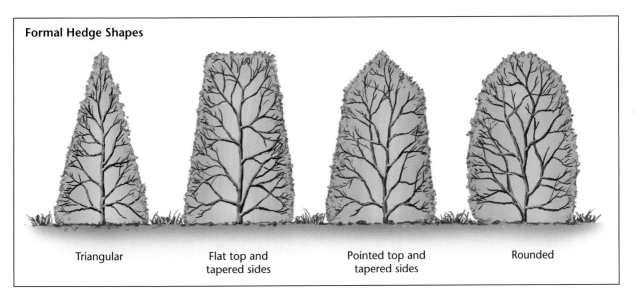

Formal Hedge Shapes

Triangular | Flat top and tapered sides | Pointed top and tapered sides | Rounded

SHEARING FOR SHAPE

If you've planted bushy, well-developed plants, the first shearing can be minimal — simply a neatening — leaving the major haircut for the following spring. If, on the other hand, your plantings are scrawny, then sharpen your shears. It's up to you to begin to encourage new growth, force multiple branching, and make the mass uniform, ultimately achieving the shape that you want.

Cut deciduous plants back to about 12 inches above the soil, leaving lots of side shoots. Clip broad-leaved evergreens about a third all around. Remove the tips of needle evergreens, taking care not to snip the leader or central stem. This trunk should be left alone until it reaches the desired height of the hedge.

The following spring, clip the plants again. In the summer, shear deciduous species and yews lightly a second time. Slope the sides slightly to create a somewhat wider base and prevent the top branches from shading the bottom (see the drawing above). In cold climates, a rounded top helps minimize injury from piled-up snow. And if a neat line is your goal, don't trust your eye. Use temporary stakes at each end of the hedge and run a string as a guide.

It's not easy to clip and wait, and then to clip and wait again. However, before you can have a tall tight hedge, you must first have a short tight hedge.

Which means not stalling until the plants have reached their final height before you start pruning.

Informal hedges require less regular clipping, but occasional touchups are essential to keep them from degenerating from casual to careless.

Pruning Hedges

Formal hedges need frequent shearing. Use string as a guide if you don't trust your eye.

Shapely Shearing

Keep the base wider than the top so that light reaches it, encouraging good growth.

Tools for Cutting and Shaping

Walk through any garden center or hardware store and you'll find a mind-boggling assortment of weapons with which to cut and shape your plants — shears, clippers, loppers, saws, scissors, knives, and yes, even machetes. You can let your eye do the choosing and buy the latest colorful gadget that proves to be useless, or you can spend some time actually wielding the products to see what feels right in your hand. Read the fine print on durability, rust resistance, long-term care, part replacement, and guarantees. You may pay more than you expected, but if you go home with a quality, long-lasting tool that's best suited to you and the job, you've made the right decision.

There are two practical requirements for a cutting and shaping tool: it must efficiently sever various-sized stems, twigs, and branches, and it must reach the area to be served.

For close-up trimming of small stems, which is what much of shaping is about, the most important helper is the hand clipper. It is available in two styles that sever in slightly different ways. My favorite is the scissors style, in which two sharp blades slip past each other. Other gardeners swear by the alternative, the anvil style, in which a single sharp blade hits down upon a blunt portion (the anvil).

For trimming thicker stems and limbs that are farther away, you'll need a lopper, which might best be described as a long-handled clipper. Again, the basic choices are the scissors-style cutter and the anvil style. For limbs even farther away — 10 feet or more — there is the pole pruner. As its name implies, this is a cutting tool on a long polelike device (typically a set of sliding extensions of wood or metal). A long rope pulley activates the cutting blades at the top of the pole.

For very thick limbs, many gardeners prefer a saw. Tree saws resemble those used by carpenters, but they

George Mendonca, the master topiariast at Green Animals in Portsmouth, Rhode Island, uses a tall ladder to trim the top of a towering curlicue of privet.

A Sampling of Pruning Tools

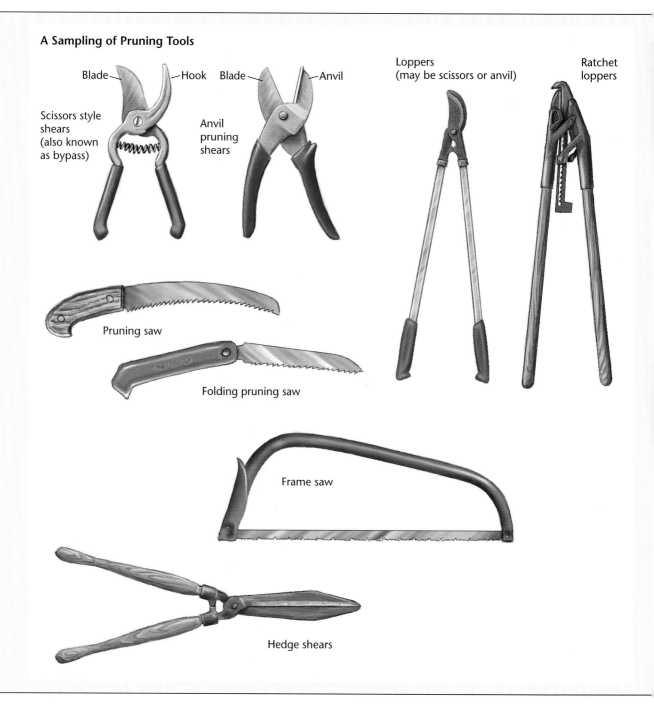

Blade — Hook   Blade — Anvil   Loppers
(may be scissors or anvil)   Ratchet loppers

Scissors style shears (also known as bypass)   Anvil pruning shears

Pruning saw

Folding pruning saw

Frame saw

Hedge shears

Spring is the ideal time to give a lollipop juniper an extensive haircut.

aren't the same. The difference is that a saw used to cut plant limbs has teeth designed expressly for this purpose. Saws used by carpenters to cut boards will gum up and stick when cutting live wood. A tree saw attachment is available for the top of pole pruners.

Also useful for severing thick limbs is one of my favorite tools, the ratchet-style lopper, a device that uses mechanical leverage to cut through heavy limbs.

Electric power tools are certainly useful, but they can be dangerous. If you plan on using them, follow the lead of the professionals: wear heavy gloves and leg guards as well as safety goggles to protect you from flying debris. Don't take chances when working on a ladder (which should be wood, not metal) and make sure that the electric cord doesn't get in the way of your cutting. For safety's sake, you can avoid the cord problem altogether by buying cordless power tools, which work on rechargeable batteries. In any case, don't work on damp or rainy days. And do keep your power tool well oiled so it won't overheat, and have it sharpened professionally so it runs smoothly and efficiently.

PLANTS FOR DECORATIVE HEDGES

Since many species of trees and shrubs make wonderful hedges, choose your plants with the specific purpose in mind. For a colorful informal divider, consider flowering shrubs. For a formal year-round screen you might choose evergreens. If you wish, mix and match species for a delightful tapestry, but be sure to select plants with a similar rate of growth and an equal tolerance for shearing. The following plants may be used as decorative hedges.

Abelia grandifolia / **Glossy abelia**
Sun or light shade
Zone 6
The first time I saw this glossy-leaved shrub, part of the honeysuckle family, it was covered with its pink, late-summer flowers, which look like tiny trumpets. Although its semi-evergreen stems can reach about 10 feet in height, the stems may die to the ground in winter where frosts are severe. Prune hedge in late winter to ensure budding for summer blooms.

Aucuba japonica / **Gold dust plant**
Sun, part or full shade
Zone 7
These plants' broad, tropical-looking leaves are tougher than they appear, and they thrive in even the deepest shade. The variegated cultivars, with their gold dots and splotches, give the plant its common name. To be sure of the pollination needed for the brilliant scarlet autumn fruit, plant both male and female plants.

Clethra alnifolia / **Summersweet or Sweet pepperbush**
Sun or part shade
Zone 4
The 4-inch-long fuzzy white or pink flowers of this midsummer bloomer are intensely fragrant and followed by prominent brown seed pods that linger through winter. Autumn foliage is a pale yellow. The hybrid 'Rosea' has pale pink flowers. 'Ruby Spice' is the only pink that does not fade to white. Clethra typically grows 6 feet tall, and the dwarf 'Hummingbird' has full-size blooms on neat 3-foot-high plants.

Low hedges and topiaries frame this lovely garden.

Hibiscus rosa-sinensis / **Hibiscus or rose of China**
Sun or light shade
Zone 9

The first person to use the term "riot of color" was surely thinking of the many flower hues in this delightful, easily grown tropical shrub. The glorious 4-inch-long trumpet-shaped blooms are freely produced much of the year. Unsheared plants can reach well over a dozen feet in height with a spread of about 5 feet. A spectacular new hibiscus hedge — some 500 feet long — now graces the entry drive of the historic Breakers Hotel in Palm Beach, Florida.

Informally clipped hedges of various sizes work well with an assortment of topiaries for a delightful garden fantasy.

Juniperus virginiana / Eastern red cedar
Sun

Zone 2

The aromatic source of cedar chests and closets, the eastern red cedar is also invaluable for its resistance to wind. The bark is a handsome red-brown that peels or exfoliates for a wonderfully rich texture. Untrimmed height can reach 30 feet. The many cultivars include the pyramidal 'Canaertii', which has dark bronze-green foliage, the bushy 'Kosteri', whose gray-blue needles have a hint of purple, and 'Skyrocket', a narrow form with silvery green foliage.

Ligustrum spp. / Privet
Sun and part shade
Zones vary

It may not be fashionable, but I've always been partial to these tough, fast grow-ing, pest-free plants. They quickly stretch to their limit near 18 feet despite the worst of growing conditions. In early summer, uncut twigs are topped with small, creamy white, intensely sweet-smelling flowers that develop into black berries the birds adore. The many versatile and handsome species include several golden leaved hybrids, including *L. vulgare* 'Lodense', a tough, bushy plant that grows to only about 4 feet, and *L. vicaryi,* which is more than double that height.

Nerium oleander / Oleander
Sun or light shade
Zone 10

The good news is that this shrubby flowering tree, which can reach at least 20 feet in height, is a stunner when covered with its 2-inch-wide elegant pink, red, white, or purple blooms. The bad news is that all parts are poisonous if ingested. If you don't have to worry about young children doing so, by all means try the many easily grown cultivars, such as 'Petite Pink', which rarely exceeds 3 to 5 feet. 'Algiers', which has dark red blooms and grows to about 6 feet tall, has nar-row leaves that are dark green on the surface and pale underneath.

Rosa / Rose
Sun and light shade
Zones vary

Those who aren't familiar with the versatility of roses will be delighted to learn that this huge genus includes many species ideally suited for border hedges or screens. Included are the Rugosa roses (sometimes called beach roses or salt-spray roses), which stand 2 to 5 feet tall on upright fuzzy stems. They bear fragrant pink or white flowers, and bright orange-red berries (called hips) in autumn. 'The Fairy', a polyantha and one of my favorites, grows only 2 to 3 feet tall and reli-ably produces a summer-long display of pale pink flowers among its diminutive leaves. Other roses notable for good repeat bloom are 'Cecile Brunner', 'Sea Foam', 'Golden Showers', and *Rosa gallica officinalis.*

Thuja occidentalis / **American arborvitae or white cedar**
Sun
Zone 3
The flat foliage of the arborvitae, which more closely resembles scales than needles, is arranged in a graceful fanlike form. Although moist conditions are considered preferable, I can't forget the plant on my neighbor's terrace, which seemed impervious to both the burning sun and vicious rooftop winds. Cultivars include those with foliage tones from deep green to bronze and bright gold. Some, like 'Nigra' and 'Pyramidalis' (or 'Columnaris'), can grow to well over 20 feet in height, but are easily controlled.

Tsuga canadensis / **Canadian hemlock**
Sun and part shade
Zone 3
The graceful Candian hemlock, an American native, naturally forms a dark green pyramid. Its soft, fine-textured needles are chartreuse-green in spring and often remain at least three years. To keep them bushy, shear young plants regularly until they reach the height you desire. Among the various hybrids are 'Globosa', which is dense and rounded, and 'Kingsville', which tends to be narrow.

ADDITIONAL PLANTS FOR SPECIAL HEDGES

Hedges for a Floral Tapestry
Flowering species make colorful and especially handsome hedges. To be sure you keep those blooms, clip immediately after the flowers fade. You won't have a strictly formal outline at all times, but that's a small price to pay for a floral wall.

Zone 4	*Clethra alnifolia* / Summersweet
	Spiraea japonica / Japanese spiraea
Zone 5	*Hibiscus syriacus* / Rose of Sharon
Zone 6	*Abelia grandiflora* / Glossy abelia
	Forsythia intermedia / Forsythia
	Santolina chamaecyparissus / Lavender cotton

A dusting of snow glistens atop a screen of neatly sculpted hemlocks.

Zone 8	*Gardenia jasminoides* / Gardenia	
	Rosmarinus officinalis / Rosemary	
Zone 9	*Hibiscus rosa-sinensis* / Hibiscus	
	Plumbago auriculata / Plumbago	
Zone 10	*Nerium oleander* / Oleander	
Zones Vary	*Rhododendron* spp. / Rhododendron and azalea	
	Syringa spp. / Lilac	

Low hedges are an orderly edging for a brick path.

Hedges for a Green Screen All Year

In warm climates, many shrubs and trees hold their leaves for much of the year, but in frosty climates, only certain species are useful for a green screen all year.

Zone 3	*Picea abies* / Norway spruce
	Thuja occidentalis / American arborvitae
Zone 4	*Pinus strobus* / Eastern white pine
	Tsuga canadensis / Canadian hemlock
Zone 5	*Ilex glabra* / Inkberry
	Picea thunbergii / Japanese black pine
	Pseudotsuga menziesii / Douglas fir
	Taxus cuspidata / Japanese yew
Zone 6	*Ilex crenata* / Japanese holly
Zone Vary	*Rhododendron* spp. / Rhododendron and azalea
	(use evergreen species only)

Decorating the Shade

Even the ubiqutious privet won't perform well with severely restricted light, so in deep shade it's difficult to have a formal outline. Rather than pine for what cannot be, opt for an informal shape and a more relaxed screen. If your garden receives at least 2½ hours of sun, here are some hedge plants to try.

Zone 3	*Cotoneaster lucidus* / Hedge cotoneaster
Zone 5	*Ilex glabra* / Inkberry
	Taxus cuspidata / Japanese yew
Zone 6	*Ilex crenata* / Japanese holly
	Euonymus kiautschovicus 'Manhattan' / Manhattan euonymus
Zone 7	*Aucuba japonica* / Gold dust plant
	Camellia japonica / Camellia
	Osmanthus heterophyllus / False holly
	Prunus llusitanica / Portuguese cherry laurel
Zone 8	*Podocarpus macrophyllus* / Yew pine
Zone 9	*Pittosporum* spp./ Pittosporum species
Zone Vary	*Rhododendron* spp. / Rhododendron and azalea
	(evergreen species only)

CHAPTER 5
OTHER SHAPELY SHAPES

PLEACH THAT BEECH

I can't quite remember just where it was that I first walked through an elegant plant tunnel, some 30 feet long. But I certainly remember that it had been formed by pleached beech trees. This is because I found myself repeating "pleach that beech." This silly rhyme, which I wince at today, turned out to be a great mnemonic device that continues to help me recall the name of this splendid method for shaping plants.

Pleaching, also called "plashing," is the weaving and interlacing of branches of rows of closely planted trees (which don't *have* to be beeches). The word is from the French and means braiding or interweaving. The result of this kind of training and shaping is a dense wall of limbs.

Depending on how it's done, there are two outlines. In the pleached form that I experienced, the tree branches had been woven starting at the base of the plants near the soil. The result was a tunnel that was virtually solid to the ground. It is also possible to weave only the branches overhead and leave the tree trunks

Winter reveals the rich texture of woven limbs in a pleached beech allee.

bare. This creates a formal avenue of massed overhead limbs that vaguely resemble a neat row of lollipops, usually with squared tops (known as a stilt hedge). In any case, a promenade of pleached trees is not your everyday walkway.

While the rage for pleached arbors predominated in the 13th century, the use of pleaching to create multiple gallery spaces, or enclosed outdoor rooms, was the fashion in 16th- and 17th-century gardens. Used in the modern landscape today, pleaching can frame a special vista or provide a splendid connection for outdoor "rooms."

If your space is minimal, use an optical illusion and forced perspective to add a feeling of depth. You can fool the eye by narrowing the space between the tree rows as they approach the farthest end. Like railroad tracks, which appear to meet in infinity, this slight convergence makes even a tiny arbor seem longer. One of my enterprising friends propped a mirror at a strategic opening.

Whatever shape intrigues you, the goal of training pleached trees is the same: to restrict growth to a single plane and get the limbs growing so closely to one another that they eventually merge or graft. It is this grafting of live wood that ultimately creates the nearly impenetrable wall that distinguishes the pleached form. Unfortunately, this does not happen quickly, so be prepared to be patient. This is a long-term project.

TIPS FOR SUCCESS

LET THERE BE LIGHT

Enjoy your shaped plants at night. Gardens illuminated from dusk to dawn sparkle with green silhouettes in summer and snowflakes in winter. For the most dramatic effect, light your trees and shrubs from the bottom up and not the other way around. Use light to accent sculptured or trained limbs by placing the fixtures close to the soil and directing the beams up through the plant.

A Pleached Allee

Step 1: Start the training formwork for your pleached allee by setting sturdy posts at the outermost spread of the space you wish to cover. Then position several intermediate posts as needed for good support. These posts should be the same height as your intended final design.

Step 2: String a horizontal wire across the bottom at the desired height for the lowest horizontal limbs. For a tunnel, the lowest wire should be a few inches

A stilt hedge or avenue of squared-off trees adds an air of sophisticated formality.

above the ground. For an avenue of trees (also called a stilt hedge) the lowest wire should be about 6 feet above the ground. Space additional wires in between, at 1- to 2-foot intervals, until you reach the top of the posts.

Step 3: Once your frame is in place, you can begin to plant your trees. When you select your trees (see Plants for Pleaching), choose young plants that are more or less identical in size. For an avenue or stilt hedge, plant them at 6 to 10 foot intervals for the length of the frame. For a tunnel, plant them at intervals of about 2 feet.

Step 4: After the trees are firmly in place, gently bend their limbs horizontally along the wires and secure them with twist-ties or other flexible ties that are easily removed when they begin to bind. Since the goal is to restrict branch development to a single plane, snip off any side shoots that are too rigid or too poorly positioned to train.

Step 5: It will be several years before your plants grow together and the limbs graft, but until that time, prune them regularly to keep the sides trim. Remove dead branches and superfluous twigs periodically, and occasionally thin the limbs to ensure that light and air penetrate the center. Feed the plants seasonally as suggested on the label of any all-purpose tree or shrub fertilizer, and water regularly.

Once the final outline is achieved, some gardeners remove the wires and frame. After a few years, however, they'll probably be inconspicuous.

> **TIPS FOR SUCCESS**
>
> **WATCH YOUR STEP**
>
> Ladders are a useful way to get to the top of your topiary, espalier, or hedge. But it's not so easy to find that solid bit of soil or paving that ensures stability. Take the time to steady your ladder securely. When you ascend, resist the temptation to stand on the topmost step or reach beyond the point where gravity is still on your side.

PLANTS FOR PLEACHING

Many tree species will tolerate the weaving and braiding required for pleaching. The following hardy species are traditionally used for pleaching, but do experiment with any species you like.

Carpinus betulus / Hornbeam
Sun or light shade
Zone 4
The elegant hornbeam is known for its ability to withstand severe pruning and is a good candidate for pleaching. Spring brings a crop of graceful pale green catkins, while autumn foliage is a golden yellow. Cultivars include the slow-growing, compact 'Columnaris' and the narrowly upright 'Fastigiata'.

Fagus sylvatica / European beech
Sun or light shade
Zone 4
This classic plant for pleaching typically has an oval or rounded outline and branches that sweep the ground. Its golden bronze autumn leaves last well into winter. The many cultivars include 'Atropunicea' (or 'Purpurea'), known for its stunning black-red young leaves leaves that turn a purple-green, and 'Dawyck Gold', a narrow form with golden foliage in spring.

Tilia cordata / Littleleaf linden
Sun or light shade
Zone 4
Young lindens have smooth, silvery-gray bark that becomes fissured with age. Its handsome blue-green heart-shaped leaves are dotted through summer by creamy white, cup-shaped flowers that are much enjoyed by bees. 'Greenspire', 'Prestige', and 'Glenleven' are all vigorous growers but, like all the lindens, are at their best only with moist, well-drained soil.

ADDITIONAL PLANTS FOR PLEACHING

Crataegus spp. / Hawthorn
Malus spp. / Apple and crabapple
Ligustrum spp. / Privet
Pyrus calleryana / Pear
Salix spp. / Willow

POLLARDING AND COPPICING

My guess is that few other decorative shaping methods are as controversial among modern gardeners as pollarding or coppicing, which are the severe and repeated cutting back of a plant's limbs to a stump of several inches. People either passionately love it or passionately hate it.

Pollarding is the term used when the plant, typically a deciduous tree, is repeatedly trimmed at or above eye level. (This is the spot originally considered beyond the browsing height of cattle.) Coppicing is the term used when the plant, typically a deciduous shrub, is repeatedly trimmed at or near ground level (see illustrations below). Although the first use of such shaping methods is unknown, coppiced plants can be seen in medieval paintings, and it is clear that the original purpose was eminently practical. The object was to produce a dense, low head with an abundance of young branches. This thicket of twigs was a useful harvest for fuel, as well as for such objects as woven baskets, wattle fencing, and poles for fishing rods or stakes for climbing vegetables.

Pollarding is an effective way of controlling the growth of normally large species of trees. Since it keeps then at a fixed height, pollarding is certainly useful when space is limited. Elegant pollarded trees have long been associated with the sidewalks of formal avenues and parks of European cities like Paris and London. In New York City, a row of pollarded trees decorate a highway near the

Coppiced Shrubs

Some shrubs look best when cut back every few years. See the list on page 112.

Winter reveals the extraordinary artistry of a recently pruned pollarded sycamore.

United Nations buildings. The resulting stumps created by the pollarding method is particularly eye-catching in winter when the trees are bare and their swollen branch endings, which resemble a cluster of knobby knees, are striking as purely architectural forms.

Both pollarded trees and coppiced shrubs are handsome additions to the landscape when used en masse as decorative borders lining a property edge. Both forms are elegant and distinctive alternatives to hedges. Coppiced shrubs are especially useful for creating an informal screen or barrier, or a backdrop for a perennial flower border or herb garden.

The pruning required for pollarded trees is traditionally done every two or three years. A yearly pruning is traditional for coppiced shrubs, especially those decorative species that produce colorful young twigs.

PLANTS FOR POLLARDING

Here are some hardy species of trees traditionally favored for pollarding.

Acer platanoides / Norway maple

Acer rubrum / Red or swamp maple

Aesculus hippocastanum / Horsechestnut

Fagus sylvatica / European beech

Liriodendron tulipifera / Tulip tree

Platanus acerifolia / London plane tree

Platanus occidentalis / American plane tree or buttonwood

Robinia pseudo-acacia / Black locust

Tilia cordata / Littleleaf linden

PLANTS FOR COPPICING

Here are some hardy species of shrubs traditionally favored for coppicing.

Cornus stolonifera / Red-osier dogwood

Elaegnus angustifolia / Russian olive

Forsythia spp./ Forsythia

Hibiscus syriacus /Rose of Sharon

Nerium oleander / Oleander

Salix alba 'Chermisina'/ Redstem willow

Salix discolor / Pussy willow

Salix matsudana 'Tortuosa' / Corkscrew willow

A pollarded tree that hasn't been pruned for some years produces long, leggy twigs.

HARDINESS ZONE MAP

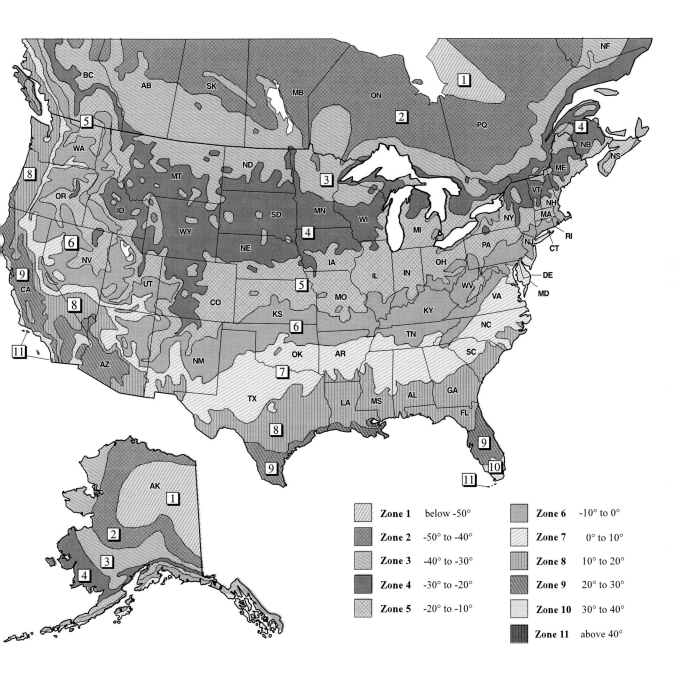

Zone 1	below -50°	**Zone 6**	-10° to 0°
Zone 2	-50° to -40°	**Zone 7**	0° to 10°
Zone 3	-40° to -30°	**Zone 8**	10° to 20°
Zone 4	-30° to -20°	**Zone 9**	20° to 30°
Zone 5	-20° to -10°	**Zone 10**	30° to 40°
		Zone 11	above 40°

SELECTED BIBLIOGRAPHY

Buchanan, Rita, and Roger Holmes, eds. *Taylor's Master Guide to Gardening.* Boston: Houghton Mifflin, 1997.

Chamberlin, Susan. *Hedges, Screens and Espaliers.* Tucson: HP Books, 1983.

Fearnley-Whittingstall, Jane. *Ivies.* New York: Random House, 1992.

Gallup, Barbara, and Deborah Reich. *The Complete Book of Topiary.* New York: Workman Publishing, 1987.

Hammer, Patricia Riley. *The New Topiary; Imaginative Techniques from Longwood Gardens.* Northiam, East Sussex, England: Garden Art Press Ltd., 1991.

Hill, Lewis. *Pruning Simplified.* Pownal, VT: Storey Communications, 1970.

Joyce, David. *The Complete Guide to Pruning and Training Plants.* New York: Simon and Schuster, 1992.

Yang, Linda. *The City and Town Gardener.* New York: Random House, 1995.

PHOTO CREDITS

Karen Bussolini: 26, 32, 41, 52, 53, 57, 61, 93, 95, 97, 98, 101, 104

Ken Druse: 2, 13, 22, 42, 48, 69, 72, 81, 102

Derek Fell: vi–1, 65, 89, back cover

Charles Marden Fitch: 27

Marge Garfield: 63 (Longwood Gardens, Kennett Square, PA)

Charles Mann: 80

Rick Mastelli: iii, 7, 11, 15, 20, 75, 84, 113

Scott Phillips/Kitchen Garden: 28

Smith & Hawken, Mill Valley, CA: 8, 17, 21

Linda Yang: 6, 14, 16, 19, 39, 59, 60, 64, 70, 79, 86, 87, 90, 109, 111

INDEX

Page numbers in italics refer to illustrations.